SO-ALM-166

HUMANITIES IN HOMESPUN

HUMANITIES
IN
HOMESPUN

by

ETHEL CHAPMAN

THE RYERSON PRESS
TORONTO, WINNIPEG, VANCOUVER

© ETHEL CHAPMAN, 1969

PUBLISHED OCTOBER, 1969

SBN 7700 0302 8   CLOTH EDITION
SBN 7700 0305 2   PAPER EDITION

PRINTED AND BOUND IN CANADA
BY THE RYERSON PRESS, TORONTO

PREFACE

The essays in this collection first appeared in a column, "From A Roadside Window", in the *Free Press Weekly Farmer's Advocate*. The title *Humanities in Homespun* was chosen, not only because it is the subject of the first story, but also because, if there is a central theme in the book, it is the reaching out for truth and beauty and the feeling for family and neighbours as we often find it in obscure or humble places.

So we have the couple living as crofters on a Scottish moor and reading Greek in their leisure; unschooled men and women who are natural child psychologists; a look at the "culture"— reading, music, good talk—that had its start in the farm kitchens of our country; a sort of elegance in a backwoods home; the fable of the good neighbour who watched over an old woman by looking for the smoke from her chimney. Our frailties are here too: the gossip, the drifter, the family that sends sons and daughters out to do the world's work, and the family proud of its closed circle.

There is nostalgia for a vanishing country life with its crossroads schools and churches, its neighbourly social hum, its woods and streams and country lanes before we had to worry about conservation; and here and there a forward look that sees another country life, not discarding the folkways worth saving but making more room for the humanities.

E.C.

HUMANITIES IN HOMESPUN

CONTENTS

NOT BY BREAD ALONE

Humanities in Homespun

On a holiday in Scotland, the president of a Canadian university and his wife went for a walk on the moor. Overtaken by a
storm, they stopped at a crofter's cottage for shelter and, as the
storm continued, they were invited to stay the night. At the
close of the evening the host said "I hope you'll excuse us if we
read our portion?" Certainly, the guests said; they would join
them. Books were handed around but the guests could not
actually join in the reading, for the crofter and his wife read
the chapter, "verse about," in *Greek*.

Not every Scottish crofter is a Greek scholar; the point is that
these crofters, whatever their educational background, chose to
live on the moor and they found their Greek good company.
Probably they had university degrees. They may, sometime,
have served society by teaching Greek or translating it; but
they saw nothing incongruous about living on a moor, perhaps
even herding sheep and enjoying Greek as another interest.

The women's book club was meeting in the home of its two
oldest members. It was a quaint and lovely place with satiny
old walnut and samplers and eggshell china and a big, square
piano, for one of the sisters had been the village music teacher
and choir leader for fifty years, and the other a school teacher,

could substitute for her in any emergency. They had retired about ten years before, but most of the book club could remember hearing them play duets at concerts when they were well past seventy, two little old ladies, dignified and charming, in flowered chiffon dresses, arranging themselves at the piano with the aplomb of concert artists, then playing like artists too —Chopin and Beethoven and Mendelssohn.

They had not played in public recently—home talent concerts had gone out of fashion—but the officers of the book club felt that "with the meeting being held in their home and all" it was only courtesy to ask them to provide the music. They might be out of practice but surely they could remember some of their "old pieces."

For years the sisters had kept their parlour organ, but when the pedalling became too strenuous, a small electric organ had taken its place in the hall. Now when the meeting was ready for music, one sister went to the piano, the other to the organ —they still liked to play duets—and to the amazement of the audience, they gave a rollicking recital from "My Fair Lady." They had not had much time for this sort of music in earlier years, but it was fun and they were enjoying it now.

In a weather-beaten farm house many years ago I listened to a country minister and a hard-working farm woman, my mother, discussing Bellamy's book *Looking Backward.* This was long before anyone had thought of radio; but these two did not find it unbelievable that in the year 2000, by "touching a screw or two" a room could be "filled with music." All of the book's prophesies interested them greatly, but the surprising thing was that they foresaw what we all see now, that social progress would not keep pace with science. They had imagination and social concern as well as intellectual curiosity, and barred from formal education by their responsibilities, they were hungry for whatever crumbs fell within their reach, through books or an exchange of thoughts with a friend.... Learning is not all in classrooms, nor great minds only in high places.

A Country Heritage

All in the April evening
April airs were abroad;
The sheep with their little lambs
Passed me by on the road.

The lambs were weary and crying
With a weak and human cry;
I thought on the Lamb of God
Going meekly to die.

The old song brings back a memory of a long-ago Good
Friday: a flock of sheep on a country road in the chill of a
spring night, the nervous "weak human cry" of the lambs,
and their mothers' comforting bleats—something of a Biblical
picture coming as it did on a Holy Day.

There were many things in the country a few decades ago
to bring us close to the Bible and to other great literature—the
sagas of Abraham and his family with their flocks and herds,
forever taking up new land; the poetry of green pastures;
prophesies of beating swords into ploughshares and every man
sitting safe under his own vine and fig tree; the parables of the
sower, of husbandmen and hirelings, of wheat and tares and
the shepherd searching the desert for a lost sheep. Such reading
was very real to us: we knew about flocks and herds and
pastures and straying sheep.

Our experiences might well quicken our appreciation of the
classics, too, since much of the world's lasting literature has a
pastoral setting. And great pictures! From "The Angelus" to
Canadian landscapes in the robust style of the Group of Seven—
how they reflect things familiar to country people!

Will this heritage, this receptiveness to something in great
books and great art be lost in the trend to industrialization?
Where, today, is there a country road safe for sheep to travel?
Older people can remember seeing flocks on country highways

Not By Bread Alone   3

but our children have never seen them. When we read "O Jerusalem, Jerusalem, . . . how often would I have gathered thy children together, even as a hen gathereth her chickens under her wings . . ." we know what it means; but would a child who had never seen a hen mothering chickens know?

At the Art Gallery in Chicago, I came back again and again to the painting, "Bringing Home the New-Born Calf," Millet's picture of men carrying a calf on a blanket stretched over poles, its mother crowding close, her eyes big with anxiety. No one else seemed much interested in the picture—perhaps no one else in the gallery had ever seen a calf carried that way. Even a boy or girl straight from the farm today might know nothing of another child's worry when she went "to get the cows" and one was missing, hidden away in the bush to have her calf.

No one wants to go back to primitive farming. The "good old days" were not always good. But they had things worth saving and some people are trying to save them. Because horses have gone from most farms, taking their style and beauty with them, some men who find tractors necessary in their work keep ponies for their children. On a farm where chickens never set foot outside an automatic poultry-plant, a child has "banties" for pets. Best of all there are farm woodlots, havens of quiet and live theatres for Nature plays. And a young wife on a hill farm says, "We may have too much rock and wasteland but we have a million-dollar view." Happily she had both the beauty of the view and the vision to see it.

Fireflies by Daylight

You must not look at fireflies by daylight," Emerson warned us. If we do, instead of an arresting, playful sparkle in the dark, we will see a drab little beetle, all glamour gone.

Years ago on an isolated farm in the North woods, I saw the night so filled with flashing sparks that the most practical naturalist might have thought it a miracle. And I heard a mother call her children, holding up the littlest one so that he, too, could see a wonder that might never come just like that again. There was hard work on that farm and few diversions; but I am sure that, because of the mother they had, the family missed little of whatever beauty was around them; that they would stop on a spring morning to listen to the singing of the frogs or to stare at the new marsh marigolds in the roadside ditch. And no one would remind them that the flowers grew out of the slime of the swamp or that the frogs were not really singing.

It is an artist in living who can enjoy and appreciate whatever bits of beauty or interest or comfort the days bring: the muted, humming sounds of a summer night, the smell of new-cut clover or lilacs in the rain, the memory of an old spare bedroom with tansy and lavender folded among the sheets. A woman whose housekeeping for her large family might seem a monotonous labour, says that she wakens every morning to some special prospect—the garden she is going to plant or the flowers that have bloomed in the night, the coming of her favourite magazine or the thought of an hour in the evening with a new library book, a pie she will make to surprise her family at supper time. She knows the grateful snugness of having the family all safe at home on a stormy night, the pride in some wise or endearing thing one of the children has done, the beauty of young love, shy and natural, as she sees it in a growing son or daughter. A worldly-wise friend may tell her: "It takes something like a storm to keep them home nowadays," or "All children go through that phase," or "Yes—but you have to watch them!" The friend may know how a firefly looks in daylight, but it's doubtful if her shrewdness gets as far with her children as the other woman's faith in hers.

Of course if there were some good reason for looking at fire-flies by daylight, we couldn't shrug off our responsibility. If a firefly were a malaria mosquito it would be everyone's business to recognize it by day or by night and to make intelligent war on it. Where evil threatens the country or the neighbourhood or the family we have to be as wise as serpents and as quick to strike. But what does it profit anyone to have a cynic examine what is beautiful or mysterious or sacred to someone, just to belittle or debunk it?

A teacher is thrilled to discover a fine mind in a boy from the wrong side of the railroad tracks; the cynic says, "You can't expect too much from *that* family." A woman from the Church makes friendly visits at a girls' reformatory; and her neighbour says, "She's one of those 'do-gooders.'" And it never occurs to the belittlers that they are the blind ones. They may know what a firefly looks like in daylight but they haven't what it takes to be moved by its beauty at night.

If Burns Had Had a Parlour

One of Robert Burns' biographers suggests that if, in the poet's home, there had been a parlour, his life might have been different in spots. The biographer was not thinking of a plush and polished "front room," but of a parlour in the original meaning—a place for guests and conversation or *parleur*.

How Burns would have loved a place in his own house where he could meet and talk with men interested in poetry or politics or philosophy however homespun, the earnest search together for truth, the friendly whetting of wit against wit! The world knows some of the hungers that troubled Burns, but little about his thirst for mental stimulant. In his limited schooling he was an avid student. Later, we are told, he was always in the circle that gathered in the churchyard after service to discuss the sermon. As a young farmer he organized community debating societies; and a friend of this time wrote: "On Sundays, between services, instead of going with our friends or lasses to the inn, we often took a walk in the fields for conversation." A cultured woman who knew the poet in Edinburgh said: "No one ever outshone Burns in the charms of fascinating conversation, the spontaneous elegance of social argument or in brilliant repartee."

Surely here was an interest that might have out-rivalled the uncouth attraction of riotous nights at the local inn. "But," Lord Roseberry writes, "with a home that can not have been very exhilarating, and with a nervous system highly strung, the temptation of the warm tavern may have been almost irresistible."

Annis Duff, book-lover, mother and one-time librarian, writing about juvenile delinquents, says: "We talk about correction and cure for these unhappy young people, but what we really need is the prevention effected by a more amusing home life. How blessedly lucky to find an amusement so constant and varied as reading!" A.D.

Annis Duff was not recommended a room in the house where rugs could be rolled back for dancing, though that might have its place, too. And Burns' biographer was not asking for a place where the poet could have his friends in for a game of cards. What they both wanted was something that would kindle the spirit, stretch the mind, and lift the thinking to a level above the second-rate and shoddy—or even above the dullness that sends people out looking for excitement.

Jack Miner had a compelling interest in birds, and as he studied and protected them he grew in mind and heart until it would be hard to say whether he had done more for the birds than the birds had done for him. He had not even had a year in school but, working with birds, he not only became a great conservationist, he acquired a knowledge, an imagination and a sensibility that made him good company for the most cultured men of his day.

A man who earns his living with a pick and shovel in a stone quarry has a leisure interest in a barbershop quartette with three of his farmer neighbours. They are popular entertainers over the countryside. Another who might be dulled by the monotony of his job on an assembly line, finds an outlet as a craftsman in his workship at home. And women—they like "self expression" too. Some still find scope for their gifts in the family and the neighbourhood—helping with the baby clinic, visiting at the Old People's Home or the mental hospital. Here they take on social skills too, while many women are losing their knack at such things.

The Old Readers Are Timeless

Our old school has been taken over by a conservation authority to be preserved as a museum piece; and when relics from its history of nearly a century have been collected, what a story they will tell! Perhaps there will be a replica of the old box-stove and the firewood, the water pail and dipper, the double seats and desks with their jackknife carving, the old registers with our names and ages carefully recorded and many more attendance blanks than would be tolerated today.

But surely nothing will be more antiquated than some of the old text books. I think of the geographies we used and of what time and two wars have done to the map of the world. I remember my British history, the dullest thing I have ever read in all my life.

But our readers! Here was something different. Sure, they look like museum pieces, dun-coloured little books illustrated with a few old-fashioned engravings; but any child who read them was exposed to a rather liberal education in the classics. And even if some teachers didn't spend much time exploring their beauty, we were required to read and re-read them and to commit so much to memory, that we carried away something to enjoy when we were mature enough to understand it.

Critics have said that the old readers were too tragic, too sad for children. It is true we read about Casabianca killed in an explosion on a burning ship, Lucy Gray lost forever in a snow storm, the skipper and his little daughter drowned in the wreck of the Hesperus, the poor little match girl frozen to death on the street, and a great many casualties of wars. There were the equally sad but less tragic deaths of little Nell of "The Old Curiosity Shop" and Tennyson's "May Queen." Perhaps the editors of our readers might have given us something just as good as these on happier themes; but anyway they introduced us to Wordsworth and Tennyson and Longfellow and Dickens and Hans Christian Andersen and others.

We were caught up in the singing lines and the dash and gallantry of Scott's "Lochinvar", Macaulay's "Horatius at the Bridge" and Byron's "Waterloo." We enjoyed Tennyson's rhythmic, rhyming stories of Lady Clare and The Lord of Burleigh. Perhaps we weren't greatly moved by the Brownings' subtle pictures of the fate of youth in war as we read about the forced recruit at Solfereno or the wounded messenger dying at the feet of Napoleon; nor by Hood's case for the woman in "The Song of the Shirt" or the beautiful young outcast taken from the river under the Bridge of Sighs. But because the poems were unforgettable some of us thought a good deal about them later.

We had a few bits from Shakespeare. "The Merchant of Venice" may not have been the best choice from the angle of prejudice, but through it we learned "the quality of mercy . . ." We had a glimpse of Goldsmith's "Deserted Village" and Dickens' "Christmas Carol" and "The Vision of Mirza" and the whole of Gray's Elegy. In our last years in public school I think most of us felt at home with "The Cotter's Saturday Night"— I am told that young people today would find it very dull indeed.

Perhaps I seem foolish about the old readers. The truth is that all school readers intrigue me. I can't see one without wanting to dip into it and I am seldom disappointed. A few are stupid and colourless, produced to order; but these are exceptions. Even in books for the very young, Milne and Stevenson and Andersen and bits from such classics as "Wind in the Willows" are as irresistible to grown-ups as they are to children.

A mother who was once a teacher tells me that her son's new "Prose for Senior Students" gave her a refresher course in English literature. The old readers could have done that in their day, too. And there's still something timeless about them.

Gentle Folk Are Where You Find Them

It was a poor part of the town, the social worker told me, and from the down-at-heel houses, whose owners certainly did not live there, anyone could see that the residents had no surplus of the world's goods.

"I often think of these people and wonder what sort of family life they have," the social worker went on. "Not that they give us any trouble. Deprived as the children must be, there's very little delinquency. But how deadening it must be to live, day in day out, in such drabness with no colour or warmth or anything to put a gentleness into their lives; no interests apart from the struggle to keep body and soul together!"

We passed a chain store and an old woman came out carrying her week-end groceries. She was neat but shabby—possibly she had nothing to live on but her pension. And her shopping bag did not seem very heavy; but cropping out at the top was a little bunch of daffodils. Evidently she was a woman who liked to have "a few flowers in the house" over Sunday.

Farther on, a lad of eighteen or so in rough work clothes came swinging along carrying some sort of mechanic's tool; and riding securely on his shoulder was a little gray kitten.

And my friend had thought there was no colour, no gentleness here!

I thought of a couple who had worked hard all their lives, had given their children the schooling they had missed themselves and sent them into the world good, useful citizens. The couple still worked as they had done for years on the cleaning staff of an office building. Coming from a Welsh background they liked music. When the children were at home the house had been filled with singing. Now they had a record player and every payday they "put by" something to buy a new record. The man told me: "When we got the Strauss Waltzes I put them right on and the wife and I danced around our living-room for an hour or more."

Truly, half the world doesn't know how the other half lives.

I remember a farm on a lonely road with a succession of tenants coming and going but never staying long. There was some tillable land but the house, old and weather-beaten, was set in a yard so pierced with rock that no one did any planting there.

A new tenant moved in one spring and in the summer the children invited me to visit them. The house was well back from the road and hidden behind a hill, so I came upon it suddenly and was not prepared for the blaze of colour before me. The whole front was covered with scarlet-runners and blue morning-glories. Between the rocks were rose and purple beds of petunias. Other flowers grew in more secluded places but the flowering vines over the gray board walls and the oases of colour among the rocks almost took my breath away. I couldn't understand how such flowers could grow in the shallow pockets of soil. "Oh", the woman explained, "John brought a wagon load of earth from the field, and we carried leaf mould from the woods in buckets. We like flowers." Work-driven as they were —and sometimes the whole family went into the fields—they cared enough for the beauty of flowers to make this effort to grow them.

The social worker had wondered about the family life in the humble houses. No doubt some of it lacked warmth and under-standing; but we find this in the homes of the prosperous and privileged too. I suggested that wealth or even "culture" have surprisingly little to do with family happiness. "But," said my friend, "there's so much to learn about human relations, especially with children; and the men and women here have never had a chance."

But I could think of fathers and mothers who had never heard of "human relations," whose ways with their children would have gladdened a Dr. Spock—like the farmer whose little boy had a long walk to school through the woods. Said the father: "It's safe enough but lonesome for a six-year-old. I didn't want him to be scared, so I took him to school the first morning, and at night I went to meet him; but I kept in the woods and didn't let him see me. That way I could tell if he was frightened. But he came dawdling along, throwing stones, so I knew he was all right; and I went back the way I came and met him at the gate. He never knew I'd been uneasy about him." Just a man with intelligence and sympathy and a concern for his children. Gentle folk are where you find them.

The Thing Called Elegance

"The Manor," as we called it, the showplace of the district, had changed hands. The millionaire who had taken over the finest old farm in the township ten years ago apparently had found still greener pastures and had sold out. No one cared very much; we had never really known the man or his family; but we had taken some interest in the traffic of visitors to the big house, the signs of lavish entertainment, the spectacular innovations on the estate—a herd of buffalo to be seen from the highway, a ski-run with a lodge that might have been imported from Switzerland, trees and hedges carved in the shape of animals. "What next?" we asked ourselves, and were awed at the thought of the wealth that made such things possible.

We were curious about the new owner and we asked our realtor if we were getting another millionaire for a neighbour. "Perhaps a millionaire twice over," we were told. "Then I suppose we'll see more show than ever," a farmer suggested. "I think not," the realtor said. "These are very *elegant* people, if you know what I mean." We didn't know exactly what he meant but we learned.

The new family seemed to know how to live with their affluence, enjoying but neither wasting nor hoarding it, putting a good deal of it to use through a family "foundation." They had a sense of fitness, too. A wall of the house that had been unmercifully wrecked to accommodate picture windows was restored to its original masonry. The painted board fences about the farm were kept a dazzling white and the lawns were smooth as broadloom, but the land was farmed as our own good farmers might have farmed it. The exhibition buffalo were replaced by children's ponies and soon our own children were friends of both the ponies and the Manor children.

Of course the newcomers had interests outside the community, but they were good neighbours so the house was open to us; and here we knew we were in the presence of quality. Carpets were deep and furnishings magnificent, but a priceless painting might hang above a homemade table, restored and treasured through generations. Even the hospitality had a special grace—we felt welcome at the Manor and our new friends came to our houses too. If elegance meant a balance of humility and dignity, good taste and propriety, graciousness and charm and the same fine metal all the way through, these aristocrats had it.

And perhaps their opulence had little to do with it. I had the same respect for another family in another old stone house of the cotter's variety, whose special attraction was its sparkling clean windows always filled with blooming geraniums. The people had no wealth and little formal education but their unaffected, gracious ways were nothing less than elegant.

A woman, who had been something of a socialite and had travelled the world over, lived in retirement in the community and once she asked the father if his son could drive her to a funeral some distance away. Later I heard her say to the father, "I don't know where your son learned his manners, but never even in my palmiest days, have I had a more courtly escort;

and he thinks of everything." The boy was seventeen years old at the time and had never been far outside the county; but he had grown up in a family whose ways were gentle and dignified —women with grace and men with a touch of gallantry that gave them a sort of elegance all their own.

How many of us in middle life or older can remember some woman, or more than one, who had an elegance—there's no other word for it—in the way she dressed, the way she walked, her voice, her air of friendliness—warm but never pushing, her conversation—down to earth when the subject required it but never loose or common. Occasionally these women had wit and sparkle, but not always. Elegance seems to come less from brilliance and sophistication than from self respect and sympathy.

We have heard a great deal about the *style* of men in public life, such as the late President Kennedy. More recently a public figure with culture, taste, poise and graciousness is often called "an elegant man." Could it be that just as we have signs of a return to romanticism in the theatre and other entertainment, there may be a growing revulsion against the crassness and vulgarity of some of our social customs, the off-beat behaviour patterns attributed to youth; that we may be coming into what the fashion designers are calling an "age of elegance"?

Beauty Is in Backyards, Too

I know what the country is like these October days: warm sun over fields of gold stubble, goldenrod and purple asters at the roadsides, bittersweet climbing over rail fences, crimson sumachs in the pastures, flocks of wild birds flying, hills on fire with flaming maples, purple oaks and all the browns and gold of the woods—a beauty to take your breath away.

But there is beauty in less likely places, too. I have a window overlooking two city backyards. There isn't a blade of grass in sight, though each house has its little square of lawn in front;

at the back the earth is packed hard by the feet of children playing. But they are not squalid places. The man in one house, on his "day off," sometimes gives his yard a vigorous sweeping. In winter time the man of the other house floods his yard to make a rink for his small boys and their friends.

There are six children in the first house, the oldest in high school, the youngest a little girl, possible four years old. It is this little girl who keeps drawing me to the window. She is lovely as a Michelangelo cherub, with shy blue eyes and short fair curls; and it is almost unbelievable that anyone so small can run so fast or think up such imaginative things to do. When her sisters, the other day, came into the yard to practise a Grecian dance they were learning at school, she followed every movement of legs, arms and curving back in a deadly serious and exceedingly comic imitation.

Last night the older boys of the neighbourhood set up a hurdle in the lane and started jumping over it. The little one watched, fascinated. Then she shot back to her own yard, found two tin cans, set them a few feet apart, and laid a stick across them, giving herself a hurdle about seven inches high. Unfortunately when she moved back and took a run at it, as the boys had done, she couldn't get herself air-borne at just the right time to go over, so she always knocked the bar off; but by tomorrow, if she continues, she'll be clearing it like a bird.

A royal family would be proud to have a child like this. Her own family are proud of her too. There is a warmth among them that might be envied in higher places.

In the other house the woman's father lives with the family. When the four little boys were babies it was the grandfather who saw to it that they had their daily outings. It was not unusual to see him among his cronies with a baby in his arms, "sidewalk inspecting" a construction project.

The youngest is now learning to walk and the old man keeps an eye on him as he staggers about the yard. The other day I happened to see the little boy, ready for a rest and a familiar lap and arms around him, go to his grandfather, who was sitting on a garbage can, smoking. The grandfather picked him up and they sat there, all by themselves. And I saw the old man take his pipe from his mouth and put his head down against the baby's for a minute. Then he went back to his smoking.

Beauty, like love, is a many-splendoured thing, and you never know where you'll find it.

Culture in the Kitchen

It's amazing how much of the culture of our country has come out of its kitchens. This isn't so surprising when we remember that for many years the kitchen was the industrial and social centre of family life; and that for more than half the year it was often the only heated room in the house.

Perhaps the most lasting cultural influence in the kitchens of earlier years centred around the rocking-chair—every kitchen had one. Some of them were "nursing chairs" with no arms to interfere with a mother's comfortable holding of a baby or to prevent other small children from crowding close enough to feel her nearness. Children heard lullabies here and stories. They talked and their mother was there to listen, to talk *with* them and to set them thinking for themselves. No doubt their questions gave her something to think about, too. It was a mutual experience in education through discussion.

Sometimes on a winter evening the couple on the next farm would walk across the fields for a neighbourly visit. Everyone felt at home in the kitchen so this is where they sat and talked. The interest and the depth and wit in these conversations varied with the men and women involved; but some of us can recall a good deal of shrewd common-sense and imagination and intellectual curiosity in the talk we heard around kitchen fires in our childhood. And if sometimes this talk was of crops and beasts and weather, wasn't that part of our culture too, our necessary concern with elemental things?

In Whittier's "Snowbound" we have the unforgettable drama of a snowbound family's evening around the fireplace of an old farmhouse. Cut off from the rest of the world they felt no loneliness in their isolation—they had resources of their own. The father and an uncle were both born story-tellers; the mother recalled interesting things she had read; a beloved maiden aunt romanced a bit about the good times of her youth; and the young school teacher who boarded with the Whittiers contributed his humour and the stimulation of an inquiring mind. Such a cast of entertainers might have been found in many a farm kitchen some decades ago.

And as a place to read, what could be better than a farm kitchen on a night when the frost cracked like pistols in the timbers of the house and the stove with its front doors open gave off heat like a furnace and the glow and crackle of an open fire? A new book was an event in those days, a luxury to be cherished. To reading families the coming of libraries was like the dawn of the millennium; but most of the reading was still done around the kitchen table.

There was music in the kitchen too: a mother singing—sometimes a whole family singing in harmony, little boys playing mouth-organs, an old man with a fiddle. Sometimes the parlour organ was moved into the kitchen for the winter, so there could be music whenever it was wanted. I have seen a piano in a kitchen, carefully covered with a quilt when not in use, but available at all hours for children taking music lessons. Physically, a kitchen with its steam from a cookstove is not a good place for a piano; culturally, it is far better than leaving it closed and silent for most of the winter.

Times have changed all this. We don't live in the kitchen now. We have books within reach of anyone who wants them. We have good music and the thinking of the best minds of our time waiting to come to us at the turn of a dial. Some of us have no hunger for these things. But here and there beside a radio or television set we may find a list of programs chosen to bring beauty and wonder and inspiration and laughter into the house, and to stretch the mind beyond the imagination of those who searched for learning years ago. Culture may have moved out of the kitchen but only to the rooms next door.

A Sound of Singing

As far back as I can remember I have heard singing. With the family sitting around the fire in the evening, or busy with work about the house, anyone humming a tune was almost sure to start a chorus. We were singing "parts" almost before we were out of the cradle, simply because we heard part-singing. Indeed it is recorded of one baby that when an older sister sang to put him to sleep, she found him singing along with her, a perfect alto harmony.

When visitors came in the evening everyone sang around the parlour organ, or later the piano that took its place. The older members of the family had musical friends—some of them took "vocal lessons"—so we heard some pretty fair singing and some very good songs. And whatever we heard we tried to sing.

Professional musicians came to our little community to sing at church concerts—our church was also our centre of culture at that time. These artists did not go over our heads with Bach or grand opera but they stretched our capacity to enjoy serious music. We heard another type of song, too. A neighbour who could not read but had a phenomenal memory for words, occasionally came to our house to borrow a pitcher of yeast or the preserving kettle; and sometimes we could persuade her to sing for us. Keeping time with the kitchen rocker she would reel off verse after verse, mostly about people murdering their "true loves," or themselves dying of heartbreak. Some of her ancestors had come from England by way of Kentucky, and we were hearing a very old type of folk song.

Of course we sang in church—at first under the direction of a precentor with a tuning-fork. The congregation followed him but they took their time about it, pouring their hearts into the old psalm tunes. Sometimes we went to evening service in the Methodist church where they had an organ and a choir and we could really let ourselves go in the rhythmic swing of the hymns.

Young people sang around bonfires, curtained in by the night, sometimes making weird harmonies but feeling close in a way they could never have felt listening to a transistor radio. In a neighbouring community the farmers and their wives were so music-minded that for winter recreation they trained with a choir leader and in the spring put on a concert that would have done credit to professionals. And they said that in singing together they had some of the best times of their lives.

When radio came and by turning a dial we could hear professional musicians, most of our friends sold their pianos. They didn't sing any more, just listened—which is not the same thing at all. Fortunately, about this time the teaching of music came into the schools, and a new generation of singers developed. Children not only learned something about how to sing; they also learned songs worth singing. Of course they brought these songs home and soon the whole family knew them. So however nostalgic we may be for the songs of our childhood, the fact is that at least our appreciation of music has improved in the last fifty years. We are learning to listen; but most of us don't have much part in *making* music. We don't know the thrill of hearing music in our own voices, or interpreting a beautiful song, or feeling the communion of singing with others.

Happily we find an appreciation of this among authorities on education. So it may not be long before we hear the sound of music over every countryside—choirs with no age limit at the top, barbershop quartettes, perhaps an occasional opera group, bands playing in the village parks on summer nights, school choirs, of course, and boys' harmonica bands, maybe a folk singing class, carol festivals at Christmastime and occasionally a concert by the best artists we can bring to our people—concerts like we had in the little country church I like to remember.

Amateur Birdwatcher

Surely one of the joys of living in the country is the opportunity for birdwatching—not professionally with field-glasses and record books but as spectators at a play, thrilled by the colour and music and movement, letting imagination fill in for fact occasionally as we follow the drama of courtship and family life, see fathers and mothers working and fighting for their own with almost human devotion.

It isn't hard to get close to birds in the country. Even if we have no birdhouses there may be a robin's nest in an apple tree or a family of downy woodpeckers in a hole in the old maple in the lane. Crossing a pasture we may see a bobolink swinging from a mullein stalk, bubbling over with song, or a meadowlark whistling from a fence post. Out by the pond kingfishers will wade within feet of us, even put on a diving demonstration. Sometimes we may be so fortunate as to see a blue heron standing on one foot, camouflaged like a bundle of sticks among the cattails; or a family of wild ducks chatting as they float along, even the tiniest balls of fluff bobbing about, practising standing on their heads in the water.

And there is the experience of looking into birds' nests with children—seeing their wide-eyed wonder at the indescribable blue of a robin's egg, their amazement at the craftsmanship of nest-building, their care not to touch anything "for fear the bird won't come back," then, after days of watching, their almost shocked discovery of a nestful of naked, gaping, squirming little birds.

There are such easy ways to attract birds to a country home.

Plant a few sunflowers in the garden and on a sunny fall day every goldfinch in the countryside will call for a snack of the seeds. Train morning-glories and scarlet runners up a wall or plant petunias in a window-box and all summer the humming-birds will be around, thick as bumble-bees. A woman writes that when the berries on her mountain-ash turned scarlet in the fall she looked out one morning and saw it "alive with birds." There were the warblers, the sparrows and finches and wax-wings and some wrens and nuthatches and vireos—all part of the great migration passing that way, stopping at the rowan tree for refreshment.

A feeding station is, of course, a winter interest, but it points up something we might well look for at other times of the year. Against a background of snow we see a bird's silhouette as we do not see it among leaves or in flight. Usually we are first impressed with a bird's song or its colour; we miss something if we do not see the beauty of line, the style and dash or the demure curves and trimness in the *shape* of a bird.

I have always been dull about translating bird songs into words. When a bird is supposed to be saying "Bob White" or "More Wet" or "Hee Hoy" or "Wait a bit," so far as I am con-cerned he might as well be singing in Chinese. But then, people tell me their budgies can all but recite the Ten Commandments —and I don't know a word they're saying. Nor can I identify many birds by their calls, except the crow and the whippoorwill —I'm never fooled on these. Some day I must get a bird book and study it. In the meantime, being the most amateur of birdwatchers, I can enjoy birds as they come, with no "guilt feelings" at being a bit emotional about them.

THE VOCATION OF LIVING

The Lone Shieling

It stands among trees at the side of the Cabot Trail—"the lone shieling," a little stone hut, a replica of the crofter's shelter when he tended his sheep in the Scottish Highlands. In Canada it seems a symbol of the lonely homes men made for themselves when they came to our wild, new country a century or more ago. We have the Scottish emigrants' nostalgia for the Old Land in the song:

> "From the lone shieling of the misty island
>   Mountains divide us, and the waste of seas—
> But still the blood is strong, the heart is Highland,
>   And we in dreams behold the Hebrides."

In effect this might have been the lament of men and women from anywhere, homesick for family and friends and old familiar places.

The little house on the Cabot Trail is only a memorial—it was never a dwelling—but it has the look of a place that had once been lived in and abandoned. We have many of these: forsaken farm houses on land that should never have been broken for farming; the remains of fires where explorers or prospectors made camp for a night in their tireless search for the gold or the waterway or the fertile valley of their dreams. It was not all wasted effort. The farmer on the poor land may have learned from his error and found a better place. The prospector may have been one of a thousand to locate a mineral bed that became a mine. And the explorer would go on exploring, no matter what happened. Kipling has him finding a veritable promised land behind the mountains and claiming not "a single acre" because in the joy of discovery, he explains, "My price was paid me ten times over by my Maker. But you wouldn't understand it. You go up and occupy." This we have been doing all through our history. The pioneers, who weren't afraid of loneliness and risk and hardship, made things easy for those who came after them.

The settling of the Canadian prairies is a story of courage and hard work and endurance and sometimes of vision—not only in the people who came from all over Europe, bringing their skills and intelligence and industry with them and giving us descendants who are now leaders in education and the arts and public life. Young men from older Canada had a part in this, too, taking homesteads far back from habitation, living in their lonely shacks more isolated than any shieling on the moors of Scotland. One of these, an Ontario lad, the keen-minded son of an improvident father, was determined his brothers should have the education denied him, so he went West where he could get free land, had a few good years along with the bad and saw the family through University. He was still alone, miles from neighbours, when the 'flu epidemic swept the country and he was found, like many another bachelor homesteader, dead in his shack. But he had broken land for the next man's sowing.

Some of the men who came to the new country brought their women. And if the privations were hard for the men, they were worse for their wives. Young mothers bore their children, sometimes without a doctor's or even a neighbour's help—and the death rate shocked a public health official into writing a treatise on "The Tragedy of the Firstborn." Many a young widower abandoned his homestead after his wife died; and the little shack stood for a year or two, the loneliest shieling in the world.

But those who survived did a valiant work of home and community building, helping each other, making such social life as they could, setting up schools and churches and presently finding a little town in their midst. Then before long the town was the centre of everything and the little schools and churches became lone shielings by the roadside.

In these days of swift and efficient demolition, no unused building is likely to stand for long. Soon no one will be left who remembers the vanished homes and schools and churches. But the men and women who built them and loved them, who knew desolation and hardship and sometimes heartbreak and who still left things better than they found them—surely they will be remembered in our history books; better still in the stories handed down through their families for generations; and perhaps, here and there, by a song or a symbol like the "lone shieling" beside the Cabot Trail.

Why or Why Not?

"Some people see things as they are and ask 'Why?' Others dream of things that never were and ask 'Why not?' " When George Bernard Shaw made this observation, he could scarcely have been referring to those "who see things as they are and ask 'Why?' " as researchers seriously looking for the cause of calamity—that seems rather to be the role of the dreamer who "sees things as they might be and asks 'Why not?' " He is already on his way to do something that may never have been done before.

A couple beloved in their community, are motoring on the highway when a drunken driver zooms over a hill and crashes into their car, killing both of them as well as himself. And a grieving neighbour says, "You wonder why." Everyone else knows why: a man who would not intentionally hurt anyone, drives when he has been drinking and the result is just what happens over and over again.

Another neighbour is so moved with shock at the driver's irresponsibility and with pity for everyone concerned that he thinks of drastic measures to prevent other such killings. "You can't legislate safety," his more cautious friends tell him. "Your plan wouldn't work." But this doesn't silence the crusader. He wants to know "Why not?" Perhaps his plan wouldn't work, but perhaps it would, and he won't give up till he finds out. Maybe he knows that all through history, what people said couldn't be done at one time was done later; and so, as the years go we make some progress.

Many a doctor before the day of anti-toxins, watching a child choke to death with diphtheria must have asked "Why?" But the doctor would not be thinking of the ways of fate or Providence. He would be trying, as a physician, to know *why* children had to die like this. No doubt, too, he hounded the researchers who, through tireless hours in their labs were also asking "Why?", until a glimmer broke through and they could say "Why not?" Why wouldn't innoculation save the children? As, of course it did.

Here is a rural slum where people live in poverty, ignorance and immorality. It is known all over the countryside that the slum is there, but no one takes much notice of it except perhaps when one of its youths appears in the county police court. Then someone may remark that that family has always been getting into trouble and it looks as if this would go on forever—"You wonder why."

But someone else gets the idea that people don't have to go on living like this. Tom and Nellie Harper lived near one of these spots and the Harpers were of those who "dream of things that never were and ask 'Why not?'" Men from "The Hollow" sometimes worked for Tom as farm hands and Nellie had been called to a few of the homes in time of sickness. "They'd be no different from anyone else if they had a chance," the Harpers agreed. If only people outside could be persuaded to be friendly with them; if the children could get to school;

if the men had work—maybe reforesting the poor land or turning it into a game preserve; if the churches in town could see that they had a mission field in their own back yard!

"Why not?" the Harpers asked, and took their case to the conservation authority and the school board and the agricultural extension service and the adult education workers who could teach men and women to read and write and make rugs and furniture just as they taught others to discuss philosophy. In a few years the area will be a clean, green place of woods and campsites and lodges for tourists and hunters; children of the men who work there will be going by bus to high school; and it will be no disgrace to live in The Hollow.

The dreamers who ask "Why not?" sometimes work miracles because they see people not as they are but as they might be. A young vocational guidance counsellor listens as a diffident, embarrassed student confides that he wants to be a diplomat or a brain surgeon or a foreign correspondent. So far as the counsellor can see he is "only an average student," and he tells him flatly that he should settle for something easier. But if the boy goes to the dedicated, farseeing woman who has been quietly "guiding" children since before the counsellor was born, she may hear him with sympathetic excitement. She has seen these quiet, thinking youngsters turn out to be giants in the fields they choose for themselves; so she says "Why not?" If she feels that what the boy wants is beyond him, she can usually think of something else that would be within his reach, and with almost the same appeal to him. A dreamer can be very practical.

Seeing What Might Be Missed

In his book, *The Power of Perception*, Marcus Bach tells us that he stopped his car on a country road one spring morning and got out to look at something he had seen many times before: a broken wagon wheel that someone had used long ago to mend a break in an old rail fence. Other travellers were stopping too; and the farmer who owned the place stood there smiling, looking from the wheel to the newspaper in his hand. He had just read that an itinerant photographer had won a thousand dollar prize with a photo of the broken wheel entwined by a morning-glory vine and, in the distance, a herd of cattle silhouetted against the hills and sky. The photographer had titled his picture "Homestead" and somehow he had made it call up a vision of the trains of settlers' wagons rolling across the prairie and stopping as they found the land they wanted, to make a farm and a home.

Bach wondered why, as he had repeatedly passed the spot, it had never occurred to him to use his camera; but he could not envy the other man his reward, for, he wrote: "It was not only photography that was involved here; it was life; for certainly the art of living includes the ability to see the unobvious; and part of life's adventure is to respond creatively to that which is ordinarily unobserved."

In a family of "normal" children there was a little boy so full of questions, so determined to find out about things that sometimes at the end of a day he had his mother exhausted. "If I didn't keep watching him he'd have every toy he owns taken to pieces to see what makes it go," she told her husband; and after one especially trying day she confided the fear, "Surely he isn't one of those *disturbed* children!"

"No," the boy's father said, "but he might be if we keep checking him. You'd better let him tag around with me. He'll take watching but I'll try to find things he can investigate without getting hurt. Maybe we should be encouraging him; when he's older get him a microscope—things like that. If his curiosity lasts till he goes to school he should learn like a house afire. It might just be he's cut out for a scientist or something."

To most people the inquisitive little boy was just a troublesome youngster needing discipline. His father "saw the unobvious and responded creatively."

In a nursing home I have seen men and women deteriorate

from alert, confident, though physically crippled, individuals to withdrawn, apologetic old people scarcely even thinking for themselves—not because of either physical or mental incapacity so much as because no one recognized them as the men and women they were. And I know a nursing home where the attendants see worth and dignity in their patients. Looking at a wrinkled old woman, bent with rheumatism, failing in sight and hearing and memory, they can see the winsome, intelligent, out-going personality she once was and still is at heart. If a group have fallen silent over their teacups a serving maid can start a conversation by such a casual remark as "When we took the washing out of the dryer today, I thought of what wash-day must have been like fifty years ago. How did you manage?"

The girl may not especially want to know how they managed their wash-days years ago; but she sees their need of an idea to set them thinking and talking.

When a young woman came as a bride to her husband's old family home she found a silver maple growing in a most awkward location, hiding the front door and throwing the planting of the whole grounds out of balance. Visiting friends wondered why her husband left the tree there and the girl herself had wondered until he told her. An adored older brother had planted the tree on his last leave before he went to the war. He didn't come back and now the tree would never be moved. Fortunately the girl understood; and the misplaced tree came to stand for a family loyalty that filled her with pride every time she looked at it. She had seen what most people missed and had known its worth—an ability far too rare among us.

The Weather Belongs to the Poor

The Irish have a saying, "The weather belongs to the poor," meaning that people with warm houses and good clothing need not worry much about rough weather; but to those with poor clothes and poor houses, a cold winter is a trial indeed. An easy attitude for the well-sheltered might be that "the wind bloweth where it listeth" and nothing much can be done about it. And it can be very pleasant on a stormy night to "stir the fire and close the shutters fast, let fall the curtains . . . pass around the cups," and feel how snug things are for us—an easy attitude not always quite comfortable.

A woman remembers that when her father bought a factory in a new town he often stood at the window on a cold night looking down toward the cheerless homes of the men who worked for him. The daughter said that at first he just worried; then he decided that something must be done and he started a crusade for better housing in the town. The tenants in the poor houses could not do this alone; it took a man who knew something about housing schemes and who had nothing to gain for himself.

In a high school district parents were troubled because their children were not progressing as they should. They complained about it among themselves and occasionally someone complained to the school board, but nothing happened and no one knew what to do about it. There was one woman in the town who understood the situation better than most. She had been a high school teacher herself; she had raised a family and followed them through school and college; with other public spirited citizens she had campaigned for good schools with considerable success. Now she was through with all that; for the first time in her life she had leisure for her painting.

But the plight of the children haunted her. She saw good teachers leaving and indifferent ones taking their places; she knew that the young man who had doubled as mathematics teacher and rugby coach was doing more coaching than teaching; she questioned the spending of money on elaborate landscaping when there were no funds to buy textbooks. She knew too that to protest might make a few enemies, but she got the ratepayers together to meet the board and she helped them to argue things through.

In a farming community where one family after another had moved away, those who were left were facing the prospect of having to close their church, a beautiful little sanctuary, rich in associations for the older members, standing guard over family grave plots with names still tenderly remembered. If only there were more younger people who cared! But young people liked to get in their cars and go to town. So when a young man came back from college to take over the home farm, everyone supposed he would want to go to a town church. And that is what he did want. But he had a feeling for the old church too and he saw where his help was needed.

So we have the man who supports state medicine though he doesn't need it himself because his firm has a plan of its own, the white aristocrats who march with the Negroes, the woman who can afford her own pediatrician but who takes her baby to the clinic so that poor mothers won't feel it's a charity service.

Even in our affluent society the weather belongs to the poor; but sometimes the privileged can temper the climate.

The Deprived

Social workers have a name for them, the ill-starred souls who have been cheated out of their right to be the best they were born to be. The sociologists call them "the deprived," and they expect to find them where there is poverty and ignorance and low morality; but the social worker, like everyone else, knows that deprived men and women may live in very respectable places.

Take a look over the congregation in a pleasant country church. There is the elder who can lead the service in an emergency. As he goes about the work of his farm, thoughts come to him for sermons he will never have a chance to preach; and he cannot quite forget the dream of his youth to be a minister —one of the many men and women with keen minds and eager hearts who were "needed at home" when they should have been going to school.

In the choir perhaps there is a voice of rare beauty. It is past its best now but there was a time when critics said the girl, with training, would make a great singer. Perhaps poverty blocked the way. She never misses a good concert on the radio but sometimes she turns it off sharply because she can't stand the frustration of hearing an artist sing as she would like to sing herself.

The friendly woman who is the practical nurse of the community is not given to such rebellion. She had that out with herself years ago when a doctor told her mother it was criminal to hold her back from professional nursing. But the mother wept and reminded the girl: "When your father died he said you'd never leave me"; so the daughter stayed at home. She lives alone now in the old house where her mother died a few years ago, her income uncertain, her spirit broken.

There are "the solitary" who have never been "set in families" and some who got into families too soon: the elderly man slipping into his place alone, too shy to make friends because his over-strict parents had frowned on even a barn dance when he was young; perhaps a man with a rapier mind and the heart of a crusader, kept out of public life by a handicap as simple as a stammer that might have been corrected; the harassed young mother of several children who never had a childhood herself because her early dates and a teenage marriage left no time for growing up; the withdrawn, humiliated youngsters bordering on depression or delinquency because they have always been overshadowed by the brighter, more attractive ones and no one seems to care much about them.

But perhaps most of us have been "deprived" in some way and have learned to live in spite of our lacks, like the disappointed elder and the nurse using their gifts where they are, the ill-equipped young mother doing her best. And some understanding friend may make the ignored youth feel that he counts for something, may look for alternative outlets for rejected abilities. (Could the woman whose rather good writing finds no publisher do the village history?) For there are men and women with sympathies quick to search for hidden talents, and to find a place for them to work and grow. They know that so many among us, born to be great, have had to "die with all their music in them."

The Need to Be Needed

At a Canadian Conference on Aging we heard of a hospital in England where, either by chance or design, a ward for old people, chronically ill, was placed beside a ward for children with long-term ailments. The old people were allowed to visit the children, and men and women fast deteriorating into senility and depression became alert and cheerful. An old man who had meant little to anyone for years could shuffle into the children's ward and meet smiles and squeals of welcome from a dozen cots. The babies, too, thrived on the attention of the old folk. Nurses had little time to pick them up and talk to them or encourage *them* to talk, so some children three or four years old could still not talk at all.

The plan had such therapeutic value that it has since been adopted in other hospitals. For both old people and children it is meeting the need to be needed.

Jim Hill and his family never stayed long in one place because Jim was equipped for nothing but unskilled labour and he had to move often to find work. It was hard for the children, never having a place in the life of a community and sometimes feeling rather "looked down on." This was not only because people in some places ignored them but also because of the way others tried to help. Sometimes women called to urge the Hills to come to church. They told them how friendly their church was and that it was important for everyone to have a "church home," especially children. The visitors hoped that at least the children would come to Sunday school. That was the way it usually worked out—the children went to Sunday school, but the parents who were shy, stayed at home. No one was happy about it.

Then the Hills made another move, and soon they were visited by a couple from the church. They said they weren't "sheep stealing" because there was no other church in the community; but many one-time members had moved away and it seemed wasteful and cheerless having a lot of empty pews. They needed people. This was a new approach and the Hills responded.

At the first service someone noticed that the Hill girls could sing and they were asked to join the choir. Soon there was a congregational supper and men with cars called for the old people who could not come by themselves. Jim had an old car and the committee asked him to bring an old man who lived on his street. And at the supper, the Hill children, sitting with new friends they had made, felt that they had arrived at last; for at their first social "do" in the new town, there was their mother taking a turn at serving and their father going around with a coffee pot just like the other men. They were needed here.

When Grandmother Killigan had a stroke and seemed to be making no return to consciousness, the doctor was troubled. "The stroke is not severe," he said to the family, "but she seems discouraged." His own idea was that she wasn't trying to recover. He knew Grandma Killigan well and he suspected she was appalled at what it would mean to her family to have a paralyzed old woman on their hands.

"We've sent for Margaret," her daughter said. "If anyone can cheer her up, Margaret can."

Everyone knew how close Margaret and her grandmother were and when the granddaughter came they warned her that she must steel herself against shock, must be bright and casual. But when the girl saw her grandmother so stricken, she simply gathered her close and cried "Whatever would I do without you!" The family were horrified; but the old woman's eyes opened and she tried to speak, tried to move, tried to let her granddaughter know she had heard and was answering.

"I think she'll get around now," the doctor said. "She knows someone needs her."

The Belittlers

"I never liked her much," said a woman of her one-time neighbour. "She was always belittlin'. No matter how much people deserved a little praise or pride in themselves Almira would try to take it away from them.

"A girl from up-country married one of our boys and at their housewarming everyone thought how homey she had made their place; but Almira said: 'She must have had a ball with all that new furniture. From what I hear she never had much at home.'

"When young Jim Trimble was made an elder of the church, we were all pleased about it. Everyone liked Jim. He had been sort of wild as a boy; then suddenly he seemed to come to himself. We had been troubled about a youth gang that was getting a hold in the neighbourhood and we couldn't do much about it; but the boys listened to Jim; and there are fathers and mothers who will thank him to their dying day. No so Almira. 'I wonder,' she said at one of our meetings, 'I wonder if it's wise, setting up these supposedly reformed characters as models for youth. What's bred in the bone . . . I always say.'

"Someone remarked about the way a woman with five small children brought them to church every Sunday, neat as pins and playful as kittens. Almira said, 'Wouldn't it be better for anyone with a family that size to stay at home with them and not spoil the service for everyone else?' "

Kindred spirits of Almira's—though they would feel insulted to be likened to her—are the cynics who never bestir themselves in any cause but are quick to belittle those who do. This may be an attempt to justify their own ways, for a man who likes to laugh at "do-gooders" may just possibly not be doing much good himself.

There are those who make light of old traditions, who see only "backwardness" in the generations before them. Ontario has two native sons, highly successful in their professions and well known as writers. Each has written a book about life in the rural community of his youth, but their interpretations are very different. One pictures his old neighbours as narrow, miserly, bigoted, dirty and not too bright. (Incidentally the locale, even in that day, was generally considered one of the progressive parts of the province.) The other man writes of customs certainly quaint by present standards, of homes without modern comforts, of people with some prejudices and limited education. But when you put down the book you have read a story of warm family life, of good neighbouring, of religious tolerance in spite of denominational loyalties, of a social life out-dated but pleasant in its day—all because the author had an artist's gift to appreciate what others might not see.

And there is the crushing belittling of the seriousness of children, the dreams of youth. A little boy who finds school difficult has tried hard; his report shows improvement and he takes it to his father hoping for some little commendation, only to be told: "Sure, it's some better but a long way from what it ought to be. Look at your sister's!" .... A high school boy has his first date coming up and with the nicest girl in school. Nothing as important as this has ever happened to him before. Most likely his mother understands, but in a teasing family it becomes a hilarious joke, until something as delicate as the wings of a moth is battered into the mud ... In an amateur opera a girl who wants a singing career gets an ovation from the audience that sets her hopes soaring until a self-appointed critic tells her: "I'm so glad they gave you that part. It always goes over. It's the catchy air, I think—an excellent number to give a young singer confidence. And you sang it very well for a beginner."

So they go, the belittlers, leaving misery behind them in a world where everyone needs encouragement, everyone needs compassion, because, as one wise man put it, "in one way or another, everyone is having a hard time."

Tea Party Binge

Mrs. Brooks awoke with a hangover. It had nothing to do with alcohol—she was not a drinking woman. And certainly the party the night before had been a decorous affair—nothing more than a committee of half a dozen women meeting to set the community hall kitchen to rights after the painters had gone. When the dishes were all back in the cupboards, the women sat down for a cup of tea; and that was when the trouble began.

Someone remarked that the Friday night dances for young people, dances with hostesses and midnight closing were working very well; and Martha Givin said she wasn't sure. The dances closed at midnight all right but who could say what time the youngsters got home. She had seen Nancy Todd and her date pass her house long after midnight. "Bill Todd should take a firmer hand with the girl," she said. "She had an aunt who was no better than she should be."

Everyone came to Nancy's defence and Mrs. Brooks said "I thought her aunt was a missionary."

"That was an aunt on her father's side," Martha said. "And wasn't she the prissy one! Wouldn't do this and wouldn't do that. Always scrounging around for clothes for 'the heathen.' If she got anything worth keeping for herself I doubt if the heathen ever saw it. The Todds were always hard up—sort of come-easy, go-easy."

"Bill Todd seems to have done very well," someone protested and Martha admitted, "Yes, but that's because he's tight as the bark of a tree. A girl who worked for them told me that when he was selling cream never a pitcher of it went to the table."

"He couldn't have been very stingy if he kept a girl to help his wife," another defender argued. "And the year she had the spell with her heart, you'll remember, he sent her to her sister's at the coast for the summer."

"He sure did!" Martha agreed. "That was the year after Sam Brown died and Bill was helping Mrs. Brown to manage the farm. Don't ask me to say anything more."

They didn't ask her. They felt she had said too much already. They were shocked and they didn't believe her; but they knew that if she kept dropping a hint here and there it wouldn't be long until every time Bill Todd's car turned in at the Browns' gate, eyebrows would be lifted all over the settlement.

The women tried to turn the talk to less personal things. One said it seemed that the workshop on vocational guidance was paying off. The Evans boy, a school dropout, had given up his job at the chain store and was back in school.

"He was a cashier, wasn't he?" Martha asked. "I wonder if he quit his job or was let out. Sometimes a boy who was never meant to handle other people's money finds the temptation too much; but a decent firm never makes trouble for a first offender —they fix things so no one ever knows why he left."

"That's what we'd expect of them," a woman put in with some asperity. "It would be a mean person who would do or say anything to cast reflection on a child's character, even if he had taken money from a till, which I, for one, don't think Jim Evans ever did."

Others took the cue and professed their faith in Jim's honesty; but they couldn't squelch Martha. When one of them, referring to a quilting at a neighbour's house, said, "Didn't we have a good time at Jennie's last night?" Martha asked brightly,

"How did you find things? I guess everyone knows Jennie's the world's worst housekeeper."

"As I was saying, we enjoyed ourselves," Jennie's friend answered shortly. Then, as a round-about defence of Jennie's housekeeping, she added: "Do you remember when we were girls and Jennie would have a party sometimes? I had never seen furniture and china and linens as nice as her mother's."

"And *there* was a house-proud woman if ever I knew one," Martha put in. "One Saturday night some neighbours dropped in to spend the evening and there was Jennie's mother, down on her knees scrubbing the kitchen floor after she'd put the children to bed. They'd tracked in some mud that day and she was sure going to have things shining for Sunday. Maybe Jennie sort of rebelled at so much fussiness and that's why she's like she is."

One of the women said that many a time she had cleaned her kitchen floor after the children were in bed. Others tried to get in a tactful word or two, but they were glad when the party was over. They had tried to keep the conversation decent but Martha had outwitted them at every turn and they felt ashamed of themselves. Because they had failed to stop her slandering it almost seemed that they had been a party to it.

"After talk like that I feel sort of besmirched," old Mrs. Bell confided to Mrs. Brooks as they walked home; and Mrs. Brooks knew what she meant. "As if we'd been out on a binge of some sort," she said.

Mrs. Brooks had a restless night, with a vague dream that Jim Evans had been sent to prison and that other distressing things were going on around her. When she wakened she knew they weren't true—though perhaps Martha's insinuations had set her wondering a little. But the misery was still with her, a mean sort of hangover from the night before.

High School Graduation

The picture is familiar to all of us—a high school graduating class such as prompted Margaret Widdemar to write:

Yellow heads and dark heads, all a-row together,
    These who were our little ones—how tall they have grown!

Hands that reach to take the world, this careless June-time
weather,
A little green and golden ball to toss for their own.

* * * * *

Some will have a dream to give and some will give a flower;
And some have only hungry hands that take and give to
none.
Some will mark the world for aye—some for but an hour;
Some will tire and fall asleep before the day is done.

They are so attractive, these children just turning into men
and women, with the fresh young comeliness of youth, their
agile grace, their coiled springs of energy eager for release.
They are less inhibited than any generation of youth before
them but perhaps no more daring; and certainly no less torn by
inner conflicts, fears, hopes, dreams and questions. Their Year
Book will predict the future of each as his friends see it, and
some of these prophesies will come true; but every class leaving
our high school this year will have in it a few great ones that
no one has noticed yet.

There is the "odd ball" who wouldn't leave an electronics
experiment to go to a school dance— to such students we look
for our scientists in a time when we need them as never before.
There is the girl who cares little about the latest mini-skirt or
a full program of dates, but goes starry-eyed at the prospect of
what she may do, years ahead, in medicine or nursing or
teaching or social work, helping to give people health and
happiness and a better way of life.

The boys distinguished in athletics and the popular girl
socialites who count on these fortes to see them through university may be disappointed. Indeed we may never hear much
about them in university. Others known in high school as run-
of-the-mill but "good students," will give the country its good,
dependable engineers and doctors and teachers, and as they go
on growing there may emerge an Osler or a Banting or a pedagogical genius. This won't happen overnight; but sometimes a

discerning teacher or father or mother has known all along that the spark was there.

A few teachers, too, can recognize the slow starters likely to pick up speed a little later. For some of these, high school may be a misery. But go back to your old school section if you have been away for forty years and see how many of them have outdistanced their classmates in usefulness, earning power and their significance in the community.

Every school has its "brilliant minds," the children likely to "go far," people say. We think "Here will be the leader we need for these troubled times." But sometimes the brilliant mind depends on personal charm or a gift of oratory instead of serious work so it doesn't grow. Sometimes the brilliant mind goes with the "hungry hands that take and give to none," reaching for money and prestige rather than taking hold of a problem and working it out.

Our schools know a lot about intelligence quotients and aptitudes but they don't seem to attach much importance to character, and history shows that in the hard tests of living, character will make or break a man more surely than anything else.

So when I see a high school class awarded the scrolls that declare them graduates, I find myself looking for things not likely to be found in their school tests. I know most of them have energy to burn but have they a capacity for hard work? They have passed examinations—and that's no mean achievement these days—but have they the intellectual curiosity to go on learning? Along with an open, inquiring mind, have they a few convictions, certain reverences that will not yield to popular clamour? With all their hard-headed know-how have they the humour and warmth and compassion that make them lovable in their human relations? Passing these tests, it seems to me, should be high qualification for first class honours.

The Stay-at-Homes

The community was proud of its native sons who had distinguished themselves in the world outside; and when they came back for Old Home Week, as most of them did, their success was the common topic of conversation.

One family came in for special attention. It seemed that a Neilson, once launched in a career, was sure to be heard from. The one who left the home town as a rising young lawyer was now a judge in high standing. The doctor was a widely known diagnostician. In his home county if anyone had a baffling illness, someone was sure to advise "Try to get an appointment with Jack Neilson. He'll find what's wrong if anyone can." One of the boys had gone to work in a broker's office and "had turned out to be a financial wizard," the home folks said; "no one knew how much he was worth now." They were proud of the foundation he had set up for charity and of the way his advice was sought by big business all over the country. Then there was the professor. The Neilsons had rather run to teaching as their first venture, but Tom had stayed with it and gone ahead; "had a list of degrees as long as your arm" people said, "and honours from universities in other parts of the world."

Jennie, the youngest, was a nurse. She had gone to the city and had "married well." "You'll remember Jennie," an old neighbour might say to another, "and how good-looking she was—and still *is*. It's something more than looks—a kind of *elegance*; the Neilson women all have it." Jennie was quite a prominent socialite—and to some purpose. The city papers often reported her part in good causes. And if old friends came her way they were given the open-armed welcome that was part of the Neilson hospitality anywhere.

"A remarkable family all through" the community agreed; and a contemporary might recall that "they were all smart at school—even those who stayed here."

Even those who stayed! Anyone who knew the family well knew that the Neilson children had all inherited pretty much the same mental calibre; that, growing up in the same home they had acquired the same willingness to apply themselves, the same honest purpose and friendly outlook. It was sometimes suggested that if those who stayed at home had left for other fields they would have "gone far." But perhaps no one saw that the "obscure destinies" of the stay-at-homes might be even more significant than the well publicized doings of the others.

Jim, who was one of the best farmers in the district, had something of his brother's flair for business. It was said he could get more out of a tax dollar than anyone else who had ever sat on the council. Living among the same people year after year, he was so well known and so trusted that they often came to him for advice when they would not have listened to an outsider. Jim wasn't a lawyer but he saved them many a grief over wills and estates and investments.

Peter taught school. While his brother, the professor, went on for higher degrees, Peter, possibly just as gifted, came back to teach near home. Thirty years later in the district high school he was teaching the children of former pupils; and being the man he was there's no doubt the good results were cumulative.

Joe and Mary, the oldest of the family, still lived on the old homestead. Neither of them had married—perhaps when they were young they took too much responsibility for the others. Now when the second and third generations came trooping back for Old Home Week, nice, promising youngsters, fitting into their ancestral home as if they belonged there, people spoke of what Joe and Mary could have given families of their own. Some may have thought it a waste, that the fine old home had been kept up just for an aging brother and sister.

They would have been wrong about this. The place stood for something in the community, for a graciousness and dignity that seemed to be passing. Mary, unassuming as she was, but with the Neilson women's "elegance," had a style that set her apart; and Joe was as courtly as any of his urban brothers at their best. Though there were no children in the house, young people came and went freely and caught something of its atmosphere. Joe and Mary had been such supporters of their clubs, the rink, the playing field, the Sunday school—had even held some serious youth forums in their own parlour that the young people felt right at home with them.

Having a doctor in the family may have quickened the Neilsons' interest in public health. Anyway the whole clan could be counted on to back any move to make the district cleaner or safer or medically better cared for. Without them the community might not have had its modern hospital or its good nursing home or its local health insurance.

And one reason why the Neilsons were such a power in the district was that they had lived there all their lives and people trusted them—not only their integrity but their good sense. It's amazing what some people accomplish in a lifetime by doing their best and staying in one place.

Failing Brooks

When Ann Benson learned that the doctor had told her grandmother she was going blind and nothing could be done about it, she caught a plane and flew to see her, expecting to find her crushed by the prospect before her. But Martha Benson, just turned eighty, was surprisingly serene. As they talked she said,

"You know the story of the prophet fed by ravens and drinking from a brook. And 'after a while the brook dried up' and he had to move to another place. When you're as old as I am you'll see that life is pretty much a chain of failing brooks and new pastures.

"Our first brooks don't last long," she said. "We outgrow 'childish things' and hurry on to make a place for ourselves in the world. As a girl I was mad about books. First I was going to be an author; then I found that my field was interpretation. To study literature and share it was pure joy. I would go to

University, then spend my life leading others into books. But I fell in love. My world was all warmth and light and a singing in the blood. I was going to be married and books went dry as dust. It was heaven while it lasted; then the brook failed. My fiancé married another girl and I went back to school.

"Soon I had back my old love of books and more. I graduated, I taught, I talked about books all over the country; and through that I met your grandfather.

"What a life we had together! The first years were crowded with working, saving, thrilling with pride in our two sons, warm and secure in our close little family. Of course we lived with books in our own house but I didn't do much crusading outside. Then suddenly the day came when the children were grown up and away. We could have been a little desolate but we turned our backs on what was past and found new things to do. Now we could afford to visit some of the places we had read about. We had more time to help with needs in our community. I found myself setting up reading clubs—in women's organizations, church societies, even old people's Homes. And I had time to read, myself.

"Of course it didn't last. Your grandfather died twenty years ago. Things happen that way. But how lucky I am to have the rest of you, and good friends—the old ones go but others come if you make a place for them. And there are always books."

"Books!" Ann flinched. Had her grandmother forgotten that she was going blind. The girl had to cry then; she couldn't help it.

"Don't fret so, child," her grandmother comforted her. "These things come to everyone. Here and there along the way something goes and you have to find something else to take its place.

"This won't be as bad as it seemed at first. I think I can stay in my own place—when you've lived in a house for fifty years you can find your way around in the dark. I'll work things out. And I'll have the 'talking books,' recordings for the blind, you know. It would be nice to be able to read for myself, even a little, but at my age I don't feel like starting to learn the blind way."

"Certainly not," Ann agreed. "You shouldn't have to."

A week later Ann had a telephone call. "Guess what?" her grandmother called. "I had my first lesson in Braille today."

Woman with a Broom

Just after the close of the last world war, a traveller stood at dawn one morning looking over the miles of rubble where there had once been a city. The outlook was depressingly hopeless. How could a place for normal living be restored from such destruction? Then, out of an opening like the entrance to a cave, a woman emerged with a broom and started sweeping. Presently another and another woman appeared—evidently they had returned to the ruins of their homes where some remnant of shelter remained among the debris; and with the tools at hand, which they knew well how to use, they were trying to improve things. The scope of their effort was limited; but even from a distance the traveller could see strong purpose in the vigour of their sweeping, and it seemed safe to predict that when the first state road machine approached the area it would be met by a delegation of women, urging that its first project be to clear a road to the place where people lived—where the need was human and urgent.

Women are rather good at such social action—seeing a problem at their doors, helping in whatever way they can, then pressing the state into doing what private citizens cannot do alone. A few years ago a little band of women, desperate because there was no school for their retarded children, started a school themselves. A retired teacher, skilled and dedicated, directed the school and a church loaned a classroom. The project spread and proved itself, so that the Department of Education felt justified in taking it over. Now the Ontario public school system provides special classes for special children.

This is only the beginning. For retarded children whose affliction makes it impossible for them to go to school or to be cared for at home, what do we offer? An institution so overcrowded and understaffed that, even though an attendant does her best, she hasn't time to feed a child who needs help at meals, or to change wet clothes, or, as one doctor says, "what is more important, to hold a child in her arms, to cuddle him, rock him, or sing and talk to him." A plan, already begun, to have small residential centres scattered over the province, might relieve the "hospital schools'" overcrowding so that they could really give hospital care to the children who should have it. And the smaller residences would offer something more like a home.

We need sheltered workshops and training centres for adults who will always be children mentally; and diagnostic services and psychiatric help so that every retarded child can become as able and as happy as it is possible for him to be. And we need more and more research into the causes of retardation and how to prevent it.

What can be done? Out of their own love and concern and heartache, another little band of parents started the Ontario Association for Retarded Children. Professional men and women joined them. They know what they are doing and their program is sound; but they need support. They need organized women (and men too) who will say to the state:

"We have done what we can with our brooms; now we need power machinery to 'get with it'. If government money can be found to build roads and armaments and show places, it can be found for a crash program to provide decent Homes and trained personnel to take care of children who cannot take care of themselves."

A Timeless Role of Women

Most of us who grew up in the country can remember special women among our neighbours who had a gentling influence on the community. We remember them for the attractiveness and the atmosphere they created in their homes, the graciousness of their hospitality, the good manners they taught their children. Some of them we remember as our Sunday School teachers. One might be a good nurse—professional or self-taught—coming in to help where there was sickness. Occasionally we had an enthusiast about music or books, stirring up singing groups or starting a library or a "literary society."

Always these women were interested in their neighbours, believing the best of them, encouraging the young people, befriending the unfortunate. Some of them had come into the district as schoolteachers or the daughters of clergymen or other outsiders, had married young farmers and stayed. Others were local girls of intelligence and charm and character. But each of them stood for something—a standard, a quality, a warmth and meaning, even perhaps a little gaiety in the neighbourhood life.

In a poem, "Among the Hills," Whittier writes of such a woman, a beautiful, cultured city girl who came to spend a summer vacation on a New England farm, lost her heart to a young farmer who was well worth it and settled into being a competent farmer's wife and more. The poet says:

> Our homes are cheerier for her sake,
> Our dooryards brighter blooming;
> And all about, the social air
> Is sweeter for her coming.
> The coarseness of a ruder time
> Her finer mirth displaces;
> A subtler sense of pleasure fills
> Each rustic sport she graces.

Country life is different now. Our level of education has risen. Our farm houses have most of the amenities of a comfortable urban home. And among our young people Whittier might find little of the "coarseness" encountered at the sleighrides and husking bees of "a ruder time." But still women have something peculiarly their own—something out-going and up-reaching—to give to the community where they live. Are we losing some of this, and will we lose more of it as we have fewer families and therefore fewer women in rural areas; as many of our gifted farmers' wives are away all day teaching school or nursing in the town hospital; as more of the services women used to give personally are being taken over by civic authorities?

The need of gifted, gracious, capable, local women in community affairs is still with us and some women are trying to meet it. Perhaps the sort of woman who, fifty years ago, would have gone to her neighbour's house to help nurse a child through diphtheria, is now the moving spirit in a clinic to immunize children against childhood diseases, talking to mothers who might not be interested and rounding up all the children in the area to see that they are protected. If there is a mental hospital in the district, such women, through their clubs, may be meeting socially with the patients, helping them to get back into their own home and community life again.

A woman who cares about old people still tries to be a friend to a lonely old neighbour; she also works with other women— and men too— to make the County Home a friendlier, happier place than it might be without her help.

The qualified leader in music or drama knows that to sing in a choir or act in a play can do more for people than endless nights passively listening to radio or watching television or movies, so she bestirs herself to see that there are choirs and orchestras and drama groups in the neighbourhood.

But how does a woman find time for these things if she works all day and has to catch up with her housework at night?

A schoolteacher and mother of teenage children was disturbed by the growing custom of children as young as thirteen or fourteen going to movies and dances in couples, trying to act an age some years beyond them. An alternative, she knew, would be to start Friday night square dances for teenagers at the community centre with mothers as hostesses. If this was to be done she would have to help with it herself, and Friday night was the only time she had to do the week's washing. But her conscience helped her with an answer. Now she uses some of her earnings to farm out her laundry and gives her Friday nights to the children. Perhaps she remembers other dances in a farm kitchen where some adored woman helped the shy, groping boys and girls of her own teen years to find their social way. It seems a timeless role of women.

Century Farm Women

Our country's centennial has brought to light some interesting stories of "century farms"—farms that have been "in a family" for one hundred years or more. We hear about the hard work and the hardships of the early years when a man took a piece of untamed land from the Crown and set to work to hew a farm from the forest. We don't hear much about the wives of these men. It seems understood that they were there, doing what was expected of them.

We may still find one of these women in the family album, in a picture taken after civilization had brought a photographer within reach and prosperity had given her the good silk dress so important to the photograph. Almost always she looks older than her years and, more often than not, the picture, like the stories of the century farm, tells something of the hard work and hardships she shared with her husband, along with some of her own.

When we look at the smooth, lush century farms today, it may never occur to us that probably once a man's wife worked with him in these fields, binding the grain as he cut it with a cradle, coiling the hay and helping to get it into the barn, picking stones from rough places—work that was usually too heavy for her. As their herds and flocks increased, her butter and egg money "kept the table," bought the children's clothes and the parlour carpet; and sometimes a few dollars could be cached away for other things. Look at the churns and butter moulds in a rural museum, and you will see the tools that gave many a public man his chance of an education.

It is easy now to forget the tragedies that came to some pioneer families because they had no medical service. The gravestones of any old rural cemetery tell the story of young wives dying with their firstborn, because there was no doctor near or because pre-natal care was unthought of. Sometimes a stone marking the graves of a man "and his wives" indicates that the first wife, worn out with work and child-bearing, had fallen by the wayside and another wife had stepped into the breach to raise the family.

Like mothers everywhere before the discovery of anti-toxins, these women knew the grief of seeing children die of diphtheria or scarlet fever when even a good doctor could not save them. They lost grown sons and daughters through "consumption" and typhoid and the "inflammation" now called appendicitis—all now pretty well under control.

But they endured these things and went on courageously making homes. They planted lilacs and rose bushes and flowers in their dooryards. Some of the lilacs, at least, are still with us. A century farm woman of today tells me that she treasures a patch of lily-of-the-valley planted by a great-great-grandmother over a hundred years ago. The early settler's wife moved with pride from the log cabin to the house of brick or stone that still stands on many a century farm; and she worked and saved to add such amenities as a parlour organ or a furniture suite of walnut and horsehair, later to be reupholstered and treasured as a family heirloom.

These women worked to gentle the new, wild country. They did not appear at school meetings but, you can depend on it, they did a lot of talking at home to get the best schools they could for their children. Later, when they had an organization of their own, they got medical inspection and music teaching for country schools. They were silent but active in the church, teaching the children, raising a good share of the funds with their bazaars and suppers and talent money. And before there were churches many women got their neighbours into their homes for cottage prayer meetings. I am told that my paternal grandmother had a neighbour who owned a piano and had some musical training—this must have been very unusual over a hundred years ago. My grandmother could sing. And whenever a circuit-rider came within hailing distance these women would get the settlers together to hear the preacher and to raise the roof with the old hymns. Incidentally the neighbour's place is a century farm now, in the family's fifth generation.

In these days when books are written about the changing role of women, a woman's need of fulfillment, how to take family life in stride without too much involvement; when women's communication media seem interested mostly in the battle with men for equality in jobs and salaries, how to be modern in morals, art and religion, and withal to be eternally young and sexually attractive, we might do well to take a serious look at our heritage from women of the past hundred years, and to ask ourselves a few searching questions.

The Hurts That Don't Heal

"Never neglect a wound that won't heal," the old doctor warned his patients. "We give an ordinary cut a dab of antiseptic and Nature does the rest. But when the patient comes back and says 'This hurt won't heal,' we look for deeper trouble—maybe a disease or deficiency in the whole man."

Troubles of the mind may come to light in the same way, the doctor explained. Some hurt suffered in the normal experience of living, that should have been forgotten long ago refuses to heal. We may need the help of a psychiatrist but the doctor in his years of general practice had learned some psychiatry himself, and he argued that we could do a lot for ourselves by refusing to let our troubles "set in on us."

In a polio epidemic, two families each lost a dearly loved child. In one home the mother refused to be comforted. She was a religious woman; but all that came from her faith in this crisis was the question, "Why did God do this to me?" Months after the great shock of the child's death should have passed, she had made little recovery. She went through the motions of keeping her house, but when she might have been giving her family the company they needed she shut herself in a room with her reminders, the little clothes and toys and pictures of the child who had died. Her other children went to school heavy with a sadness and a fear they could not understand. Her husband lost heart in his work—at home there was something he could not cope with however he tried. And the woman herself ultimately had to go to a mental hospital for a while.

In the other house the striken family wept together—and freely, sharing their grief, comforting each other. Said the mother: "I felt so sorry for my husband—he seemed to feel he had to carry the load for all of us; and the children—you can't expect children to understand death; so I had to pull myself together and do what I could for all of us. I had always thought I believed in immortality. Now that I desperately needed to believe, I talked with others whose faith was strong; drew assurance from every source I could trust. And what a light came through when we looked for it!"

We have all known personalities deformed by carrying grudges. A man wants the nomination for a public office; someone pulls a string and gets it away from him and he never forgets it, never loses a chance to get in a word against his one-time competitor. Forty years later people wonder what ails the old man, to make him so bitter.

Lisa Temple, an intelligent and lovely girl, was as shattered as anyone would be when her fiancé broke their engagement and married another girl. Lisa could barely remember her great-aunt Melissa, a queer old woman, forever talking about a tragedy of her girlhood as if it had happened yesterday. In the words of her day, Melissa had been "jilted" by her lover; and it had left her "heart broken." For the rest of her young life, Melissa reported, she had shut herself away from the world —never went to a party, never looked at a young man though there were those who cast their eyes in her direction. She had fully expected to "go into a decline" but she had survived—the tolerated, eccentric maiden aunt, filling her life with odd jobs for the family wherever she was needed. And she had never spoken to "him" again.

Lisa's way was different. When she had had time to get herself in hand, she could say to her friend—and mean it: "How fortunate for both of us that you saw your mistake in time!" She never thought of going into hiding. A change of associations would be good of course, and she would find this in the university work she had given up to be married. And she never doubted that some day she would find a greater love than the one she had lost, because she would be wiser about it.

Misfortune, rejection, grief and failure—these come to all of us; and indeed we suffer from them. But in a healthy, outgoing life they don't last long. Perhaps, too, they build the resistance we need against some major attack that might wreck us. The great souls with endurance and courage, compassion and cheer, have never had things easy.

A Flair for Kindness

It was Farm and Home Week at Cornell University, an event that brought people from all over the state for a week of extension work; and between sessions the visitors did a good deal of walking from one college building to another. Cornell campus is hilly and in this midwinter season it was well spotted with ice; travellers were glad to use the handrails along paths on the steepest slopes.

One elderly couple had their crippled granddaughter with them. She could not walk so they took her from one hall to another on a hand-sled. On an afternoon when these people were labouring up a hill, the one on the inside of the path clutching the rail, but both finding it difficult to pull the sled and keep their footing, a half dozen young men came tearing out of a students' residence and went running and sliding down the hill, "youping and yelling" like madmen. Perhaps they were letting off steam after hours of hard study, but to some of the visitors who stopped to stare after them they must have seemed so many young wastrels playing away their precious time at college.

Once started, there was no way of stopping in their precipitous descent, but the instant they reached the bottom of the hill two of them dug in their heels and started up again, in the direction of the footpath. They overtook the couple with the sled, took the rope from them and drew the sled to the top of the hill and on to the lecture hall. After this, other surefooted people were ready to help—they just had not thought of it before. The students had a flair for seeing the thing to do and doing it.

At a hotel in the Southern States a young father and mother came in for dinner with two small boys and a very young baby in a basket. The mother looked exhausted. Probably they were having dinner out to give her a rest; but it wasn't working very well. The baby cried and nothing the woman did seemed to comfort it. The man tried to be as helpful as he could, taking care of the little boys, looking his sympathy; but the little one, possibly responding to its mother's tired nerves, cried harder and harder.

Then a waiter who seemed to be in charge of that corner of the room came over. "Let me help," he said. He was a Negro, an old man with grizzled hair and a very dark, wrinkled, intelligent face. He took the baby with the ease of one who has handled many babies. His arms making a cradle, his capable old hand with a serviette shaping a headrest, he walked back and forth mumbling something the baby seemed to understand, for its crying quieted. The family went on with their dinner; and the baby went to sleep. When the couple told the steward about it he wasn't surprised. "The old man sees things to do," he said.

Then there was the teacher at a school commencement, who suddenly saw that when the awards were made one child of the whole school, a boy already close to discouragement, would not get a prize, a teacher who could think to write a cheque and a note telling the chairman, to say that "because of sound judgment shown in many ways," the boy was being given the unprecedented privilege of choosing his own book.

It's a most attractive trait, this flair for kindness.

Passive Resistance

Sarah Meyer had a Quaker background, so she had heard about meeting the forces of evil with "passive resistance." She had never had to resort to this in conflict with the law, but she had often found it effective in her personal affairs.

Looking over the paperbacks in the drug store one day, Sarah found a friend dipping into a book with a very lurid cover. The woman put the book back on the rack as if it had suddenly burned her fingers.

"Isn't it a disgrace," she said, "that our young people have to be exposed to stuff like this?"

"There are some good books among them," Sarah said. "I'm looking for *Vanity Fair*. All my life I've heard about it, but somehow I've missed reading it. I find a lot of the classics here."

"But look at this!" the woman went on, indicating a title that promised a treasury of obscenity and violence. "I found my own boy reading one of these and I took it right away from him and burned it."

"Were you able to give him something to take its place?"

Sarah asked. She remembered when her son was growing up, turning the mattress on his bed one day and finding a book hidden there. She had left the book where she found it—it was a rule in her family that the individual's privacy must be respected; but that very day she searched the library for books good enough to outweigh the attraction of the second-rate. She left them about where the boy would find them for himself; and, as she expected, he read them and went to the library for more of the same sort.

Sarah had a built-in serenity, very resistant to small hurts or embarrassments. No doubt she was shocked when risqué talk came her way, but so far as anyone could tell, it simply didn't reach her. She didn't frown or smile or give any sign that she had heard it, so the point was lost completely. What was intended to spark hilarity or protest fell into an uneasy silence, most discouraging to a story-teller. With the same response—or lack of response—she could stop a piece of slander dead in its tracks.

Once Sarah was mistress of ceremonies at her travel club's family night; and the speaker, authentic and entertaining with his travelogue, turned out to be very free-wheeling in his casual comments. At one point, wondering just how far he dare go, he turned to Sarah and asked if he might tell a story. He may have been surprised when, entirely unflustered and friendly, she replied, "I'm sure a story of yours would be worth hearing; but if you're in any doubt we don't mind missing it. We're enjoying your pictures." So he went on with his lecture.

Where Sarah lived, the young people and the children went to the movies on Friday nights and Saturdays; and the only theatre in town showed pictures that had the parents worried. Some of the mothers banded together to launch a public protest; and while Sarah agreed that something should be done, she felt that this sort of attack would only advertise the bad pictures. "Besides," she argued, "what have we ever done to get something better? Do we ever patronize a good picture? I know I haven't been in the theatre for years."

They found that a Disney picture was coming and, to the amazement of the management, a good representation of the "solid" citizens of town came to see it. The next week the film was the usual crime story, reeking with lechery and violence; and again the most decorous matrons in town were there. They walked out after the first few scenes, found the manager and told him what they thought of his show. They threatened to expose it in the local paper but the man was not worried—he knew that if the picture was attacked in the press, people from all over the district would flock to see it.

Sarah had another plan, and the women delegated her to explain it to the agent. She told him that the women felt the children should have an alternative to his movie fare, so they were opening a "teen town" for Friday nights and Saturdays. It wasn't fair, he protested. He had to take the bad pictures with the good. "I've no doubt you have your problems," Sarah sympathized; "but if you let us know when you have something good coming, we'll publicize it for you. If it's good enough we might give up our party for the night so the children wouldn't miss it." The town has quite a good movie program now.

On Getting Involved

There's something very up-to-the-minute in the story of the man who was robbed and beaten and left half-dead at the side of the Jericho road. Passersby saw him lying there, but they kept well to the other side of the road or if, out of curiosity, they stopped to look, they hurried right on again. No doubt they had pressing business of their own to attend to, and they didn't want to "get involved." Besides, the thieves might still be lurking about waiting for another victim. So the traffic continued as usual while the injured man's condition worsened. Then a man came along who "had compassion"; and we know the rest of the story.

The drama of the Jericho road seems to be having a revival. A crowd of people watch a policeman being beaten by thugs and no one interferes. Some of the onlookers might not be very effective in a street fight, but no one even phones the police for help.

One night a pilot flying alone crashed in a field near a high-way. Miraculously he crawled out of the plane, alive but terribly cut about the head with flying glass. He got to the road and tried to flag down a car; but when the headlights flashed on a man covered with blood, every driver stepped on the accelerator and got away as fast as he could.

A child dies from neglect and cruelty, and in the investigation that follows, neighbours testify that they heard beatings, they suspected the child was suffering from hunger and fright. Some of them had felt that the authorities should be told about it; but one hesitates to inform on a neighbour, and with people like these there might be reprisals.

But the good Samaritans are still with us. A boy of fourteen goes on trial for murder because he is the last person seen with the victim. He is sentenced to be hanged, later this is commuted to life imprisonment, so he spends his youth in prison, pretty generally forgotten. But a woman who is a writer believes the boy is innocent and she sets to work to put the truth before the public. The article she started grows into a book; but no Canadian publisher will take it—a business does not enter lightly into conflict with a court of law. Finally a publisher is found in Britain and *The Trial of Stephen Truscott* stirs the conscience of Canada to ask for an inquiry. Isabel Le Bourdais didn't know her book would be a best seller. She wrote it in the face of about every possible discouragement, because she cared about a boy left to die by the roadside. She didn't worry about "getting involved."

We find this courage in more everyday affairs. A child falls into the water or a swimmer is caught with a cramp. Perhaps no friends are near to hear the cries for help. But how often an unidentified stranged comes to the rescue! When he gets the victim to land people have gathered to give first aid and by the time this excitement is over the rescuer has disappeared.

A few vigilantes are still among us. There are men and women who don't hesitate to knock on the door where a child is being abused or to alert the Children's Aid to keep an eye on a family; who would be just as quick to engage with exploiters of youth or age or the disadvantaged in any way.

There is the woman with the heart to check a gossipy slander wherever she hears it; the man so devoted to a good but unpopular cause that he votes alone, year after year, and dies before the time when everyone approves it. And there are the crusaders not afraid to get involved in outright fighting for reforms that would make wrongs endured today, impossible tomorrow.

There's a legend that a few days after the Samaritan had taken care of the first man he found on the Jericho road, he came that way again and found another robbed and beaten in the same way, evidently by the same gang of thieves. He took care of this man too. But when he met the same situation a third time, he called a meeting of his neighbour Samaritans and they got out their old muskets (or their equivalent in that day) and set out to clean up the Jericho road.

The Caution of a Cat

"A cat that has once sat on a hot stove will never sit on a cold one." When Mark Twain wrote this no doubt he was thinking less of cats than of humans.

Evidently Nature has given a cat a mentality that is capable of caution. An unpleasant experience is so recorded in memory that a cat will avoid a similar catastrophe for the rest of his life—even if it means missing a nice, cool perch on a hot day on a pile of old stoves in a scrap-iron shed. Through whatever means of communication cats have, a singed one would probably convey to others that "you can never trust a stove. Nine times out of ten it's hot. And the warmth that feels so good when you sit under the hearth is a devilish 'come-on' to lure you to your death or worse."

We have all seen such fixed ideas in people. Speaking of a race or a "class" we hear men say: "Oh yes, they're clever—and pushing. They'll get to the top no matter who is trampled on the way. You say they 'keep the law'; that's because they're too smart to get into trouble. And they may be 'devoted to their families'. But I was fooled by one of them twenty years ago and I've had no use for them since."

A family—call them "the Griffins"—in one of our early settlements establishes a reputation for petty thieving, shiftlessness and illiteracy. As the old men die off, their sons and daughters gradually take on habits of honesty and industry. Their children go to school for a few years and learn to read and write. A few more generations and the children get to high school. Some of them marry into the most respected families in the district. But there are a few old neighbours who can't forget their background. "Once a Griffin, always a Griffin," they say; and they revive records of the time when great-great-grandfather Griffin was on trial at every sitting of the county court and spent most of his time in jail. So now, if a young Griffin is especially brilliant or able it is usually better for him to move to another part of the country where he will be accepted for what he is.

There are the men and women who cling to a grudge as if it were a moral principle. In the private history of a rather illustrious Canadian family there is a story of a girl, Sally, jilted by a young man who then married her sister. Sally never spoke to him again. Even though she later married his brother and they were continually meeting at family gatherings, she brushed past him as if to say: "I've been hurt once and I'm taking no more chances." It was awkward for other members of the family and highly amusing to the young ones. A great-great nephew thought it must be very flattering after forty years to have a woman still feel injured because you hadn't married her. Sally might have saved her own dignity and spared everyone else a lot of embarrassment if she had "never let the sun go down on her wrath."

Mark Twain's cat would never lose its life through curiosity; would never put out an exploratory paw to touch the edge of the stove or bring his face close, like a woman testing the heat of a flat-iron. He would never reason: "With all its dangers, this stove is a good thing. It keeps the kitchen snug on winter nights. Maybe with a little encouragement someone will make a stove that will warm the whole house." The cat had a closed mind and nothing in common with the inventors, the explorers, the researchers and the pioneer souls brave enough to work for a cause while it is still unpopular. A crusader was never held back by caution.

A Kind of Valour

In *Pebble in a Pool*, Elizabeth Yates' biography of Dorothy Canfield, brilliant writer and a woman of rare beauty and strength of character, we read: "Dorothy is like a bright flame in a sturdy iron lamp. She is like the elm in the hill pasture. She is the result of the influences around her *as well as standing up to them*." The author might have added that Dorothy is like other individuals here and there who, in standing up to forces that might have destroyed them, have developed a fibre and a quality they might never have had if they had lived all their lives in fair weather.

In the early days of the Canadian West, a bride came from the East to homestead far from neighbours; and she was lonely. After a while the loneliness became strangely frightening. She found herself staring out at miles of wheat and miles of sky and listening for footsteps that never came. When she heard that a woman on a homestead farther back had been taken to the hospital, insane from loneliness, she said to her husband, "I've got to see the neighbours."

She rode a horse six miles to the nearest homesteader's shack and found a woman as lonely as herself. She searched out other women—some had come from Southern Europe and could speak no English; but with their common need and their young neighbour's encouragement they became fast friends. More people moved in and a school was built; then the people worried about their children growing up in a place where there was no church within travelling distance. The woman from the East worried too, got the settlers together and started a worship service in the school house. As the children grew into young men and women with no leisure interest beyond all-night dances, she led them in a debating club. And all the time, as she struggled with her problems, the woman grew—grew in friendliness and foresight and fortitude. It was not surprising that years later her people chose her to represent them in parliament.

The influence of a good home is generally appreciated; the good that may come from "standing up to" the influence of a bad home is not so well known. Yet orphans and others who grow up unloved and unwanted sometimes make wonderful fathers and mothers, because they are determined their children shall not suffer as they did. And I think of the sons of a man who made life a misery for his family by his fits of temper and drunkenness and cruelty. At these times his language went the limits of profanity and obscenity; and one might have expected some of this to rub off on his sons, in spite of the qualities they had inherited from their mother. Instead of this, they found their father's behaviour so revolting that they would have none of it in themselves. Because they had had no opportunity for education the boys' first jobs took them into the rough life of mines and lumber camps. They were physically tough and could take care of themselves in a camp row if they had to; but a foreman said: "They never touched liquor even when there was enough of it around to float a ship; and their language would have got by at a prayer meeting.

So the theory that we are products of the influence around

us is not entirely sound. As a child, Dorothy Canfield, like everyone else, would be marked indelibly by the influences of her environment. As a woman she either accepted or "stood up to them."

Rehabilitated

Mary Moore was going home from the hospital and she was frightened. She could remember, though vaguely, the turning away from friends, the weeping in public, all a part of her breakdown, and it was not easy to go back.

But she was well now and going home. She had not seen the boys, only six and ten years old, since she left them; but Jim, her husband, had been a faithful visitor, devoted and encouraging. He could not forgive himself because, before he understood her trouble, when she wakened him, crying in the night he had told her she "must snap out of it," when she could no more have stopped crying than a consumptive could stop coughing. As she recovered she wanted to talk to him about her sickness, to try to explain; but he was afraid this might upset her, so he said, "It's all behind you now. Don't think about it."

Another regular visitor was her Aunt Sarah and Mary *could* talk to her. She listened with an intelligent curiosity. "Seems very much like I felt when I was delirious with the 'flu," she would say. "I guess most people have had some experience with it." Sarah had been "studying up on" mental trouble. She informed Mary that one person in ten suffers some emotional disorder, and she knew the great minds in history who had their spells of delusion.

Sarah had some advice for Jim, too. When he told her he was going to send the boys to his mother's for a few weeks so Mary could "take it easy for a while," she was really alarmed. "Besides," he said, "they're sure to ask questions."

"And why not?" Sarah demanded. "Naturally they'll want to

know why their mother left them; and she'll be able to explain to them better than anyone else. Mary is *well*; if she weren't the doctors wouldn't let her come home. Then we've got to act as if she were well. We've got to help her to have faith in herself. And don't be urging her to 'take things easy,' as if she were still sick. What she needs is warmth and companionship and someone depending on her. Instead of telling her to rest while you get supper, say: 'Could we have an apple pie for supper? We haven't had a pie since you went away.' That's a way of saying, 'It's good to have you home.'"

It would be hard to say how much Sarah saved her niece by dropping a word here and there to her friends. When the church women planned a tea to welcome Mary back, Sarah thought it might be better to be more casual about it. So instead of asking her to face the whole community at once, her friends found ways of seeing her singly or in twos or threes at their homes or hers.

Two shy little thirteen-year-olds called to ask if she would take their Sunday school class again. Mary almost panicked; but Sarah said, "Have them in for supper to talk it over and see how good it feels to be together again." It was an easy first step back into the community.

Best of all, she was back with her family. The boys seemed to have forgotten her illness. But one day the little one whispered, "You'll never go away again, will you?" And holding him tight she said, "No. I'm sure I'll never have to go away again."

You Can't Go Home Again

The tourist season was over and only a skeleton staff stayed for a few days to close the lodge for the winter. There was the owner, Mary Lane; Katie, the head waitress, a school teacher from Saskatchewan; Olaf, the young Dane who had come from the city to build cabins; and old Mrs. Rennie who, for the last twenty summers, had overseen the laundry and kept the linen mended.

The northern nights were chilly and, while Mary worked in her office, the others sat in the warm kitchen. They needed the warmth of companionship too, for they were all lonely and homesick—homesick for something they could not go home to.

The woods made a blaze of colour over the hills—"the prettiest I ever see," said Mrs. Rennie. Olaf took picture after picture to send to his Karen in Denmark; but the girl from the West said: "I'm thinking what it must be like on the prairie now—miles and miles of gold wheat stubble; sunsets that take your breath away, a nip of frost in the air and the wild ducks flying low over the sloughs."

"You'd like to go back, wouldn't you?" Olaf asked her gently, for he knew why she wasn't going back. She had been going to marry a neighbour boy. At a dance last winter he had met a girl he liked better. They were married in the summer; and that was why Katie had come to Ontario.

"There are times when you can't go home again," she said.

Olaf considered this. "I don't know," he said. "If you came away to escape seeing a man you loved with another girl, maybe that was good sense. But no man has a claim on the fields and sunsets over the whole prairie, or on the heart of more than one woman. You love the West. Go back to another part of it; teach another school; maybe get to love someone finer than anyone you've known yet. You *can* go home again."

"Then what about you?" Katie came back at him. "Why don't you go back to Denmark?"

"I wouldn't need to go back to Denmark to be at home if Karen were *here*," he said. "I came first to get a home together, but it takes so long. Wages are good, yes; but costs are high— and every week is like a year."

"You're no wiser than Katie," Mrs. Rennie told him. "You're a good carpenter; your girl's a nurse. A carpenter and a trained nurse need have no fear of want in this country. You send for

Karen now. If you don't, lonesome as you are, you might take up with someone else. Wouldn't that be a fine end to your dreams! If I were young I wouldn't let things beat me so easy."

This was Mrs. Rennie's last summer at the lodge. She would go back to her room in the city and it was hard to face the bleakness ahead. She said:

"I always thought when I got too old to work I'd go back to the place where I was young and take up with my friends again; talk over old times, lend a hand where I could help, drop in to sing the old hymns in someone's parlour on a Sunday night. So I went to look things over. Some of my old friends lived with their children; some were in the Home; but most of them were dead."

The young people could scarcely imagine a situation like this. Out of her sympathy Katie said: "There must be many people who have lost their friends just because time passes, if we knew where to find them."

Mrs. Rennie knew where to find some of them. They met in little groups here and there in clubs and churches. She had even heard them singing the old hymns as she passed on a Sunday night, but she had never thought of joining them. Now she wondered if some of them might be lonely too. She said:

"Maybe it's never too late to make friends. I guess if you can't go home again you try to make a home somewhere else."

Then Mary Lane came to make coffee and to break the sad news that her land was being taken over for a new park.

"But the lodge!" the others said. "Whatever will you do?"

"I'm looking for another site," said Mary. "I'll build again."

Day-tight Compartments

Ellen Evans was a "tower of strength" to her family and friends —partly because of her ability to cope with things that made other women depressed or frightened, partly because her serenity was contagious. People who knew her well said she "could do two days' work in one if she had to, and make no fuss about it"; that she "hadn't any nerves"; that, "the way she lived, you'd think every day was a special occasion."

Life had not been easy for Ellen. She had raised six children of her own and mothered several others through emergencies. She could hear the first whimper of a baby's cry in the night, attend to his needs and go right back to sleep—perhaps she had schooled herself to this, knowing that a wakeful night is no preparation for the day ahead. When her son was stricken with an incurable illness, she set herself to make each day as happy as she could for him. He had played in a neighbourhood orchestra, and people passing the house often heard Ellen singing at her work to the accompaniment of his guitar. When his young friends came to see him, nervous at the prospect of death, fearful of saying the wrong thing, they might be surprised to hear his mother say, "Can't we have some music?" She was never unaware of the grief and loneliness ahead; but she knew she could take it as she had taken other heartbreaks; and she must be strong to help the family through.

Perhaps Ellen had never heard of Dr. Osler's warning that "The load of tomorrow, added to that of yesterday, carried today, makes the strongest falter"; and his admission that the only way he could carry the responsibilities of his work was "to keep each day in its own day-tight compartment." But that was Ellen's way of living, too.

So, because each new day came like an empty cup to be filled, and disappeared forever with the night, it seemed important to Ellen to make something of it. She was one of the happy sort who waken to their day's work expectantly, eager to be at it. If Ellen had kept a diary, it might have shown a purpose sharpened by her sense of the preciousness of time. A day's entry would be likely to carry something of service and enjoyment and beauty, such as: "Finished planting the garden today. Went to town and found the special pattern Mary wants for her graduation dress. Brought Aunt Nettie out to the farm for a holiday—her memory is failing but she feels at home here.

Saw what I'm sure are the same pair of robins that came last year, building their nest in the crab-apple tree." . . . And she would not waste the night worrying for fear the garden might wither from drought; or the graduation dress might not be as pretty as its picture; or Aunt Nettie might lose her memory altogether; or a cat might climb the crab-apple tree.

Ellen had no patience with a high school system that presses its children into sports and dances and hobby clubs, then goads them into cramming for examinations; or with a child's habit of mixing homework with a favourite TV program. "You have to learn how to use time just as you learn to use money," she told her family. "The early part of the evening is to be kept for homework all through the year. Work hard while you're at it; and when you've done all you can for the day, put your books away and forget them. Sing or dance or have "a piece" to eat. Then go to bed and rest. Tomorrow is another day."

To Stand and Stare

The birds that came to the feeding station in the Weavers' backyard were having a thin time of it. It was the most up-to-date station for miles around—a wide tray set high on a metal pole out of reach of cats; and every morning Jennie Weaver laid out a good day's rations of the seeds and suet the birds needed to keep heat and strength in their little bodies. But something had gone wrong. No sooner had Jennie disappeared in the house than a squirrel, not satisfied with his own hand-outs, grappled his way up the pole, scattered the birds in all directions, gobbled up most of their food and carried the rest away in his pouches.

Of course such skull-duggery couldn't go undetected forever. One day Jennie heard a commotion among the birds and looked out in time to see the squirrel in possession of the feeding tray. When she opened the door he took a flying leap to the ground, landed in the soft snow and escaped unhurt. The descent from the feeding station was no problem. What the Weavers wanted to know was how he got up there.

The next day Jennie spread the birds' table as usual and watched. Birds flew in from all directions; and in no time at all the squirrel appeared on the ground below. He got his arms around the pole and began to climb. It wasn't easy—the smooth metal gave a poor foothold; but he was determined and, by this time, fairly experienced. He advanced with never a downward slip, climbed onto the tray and sent the birds flying.

The next day Tom Weaver used a little strategy of his own to protect the bird-station—he greased the pole. The bird feed was put out as usual; then from the window the Weavers watched a drama such as they had never seen before. The squirrel came bounding across the yard, caught the pole two feet from the ground and came down like a man on skis. His consternation was very evident. Nothing like this had ever happened to him before. He looked furtively about, his coat fluffed, his tail twitching. He sniffed at the pole without touching it, sniffed also at the scent of the smorgasbord above and decided to try again. He clutched the pole and strained upwards, but nothing happened. He tried making a spring to get started, but the moment his feet left the ground he came down again. Finally he sat down in the snow perhaps to think things over; but by this time the birds had cleared the table and there was no point in climbing the pole anyway.

The squirrel was not easily discouraged; he came back every morning and as some of the oil on the pole was worn off by the weather and his own fur he made a little progress. The Weavers took time to watch him. Often out of pity for his frustration they tossed him an extra snack to divert his attention. They seemed to know that in the strain and stress of life for squirrels or humans, diversions are important.

For the Weavers were serious folk. They did not live to themselves. They followed the events of the world through the press and radio and television, with the honest concern and frustration of thousands of their kind. They tried to find where their own responsibilities lay. They supported the United Nations and the crusades to save the children and feed the hungry over the world. They were devoted to their church and distressed by the controversy among its high officials over doctrine and ecumenism, debaters attacking one another with the sarcasm of adversaries in a police court. The Weavers had children and grandchildren—their family had been the joy of their lives. Now scarcely a day passed without some radio reference to "the conflict of the generations," and panels of men and women urging youth to rebel at the "old moralities."

No one seemed to take much notice of anything that might give comfort or courage for the day's need; but the Weavers knew that some of these comforts were the elemental, timeless things right at their own door. They had worked hard all their lives but even at their busiest they could have said: "What is this life if full of care we have no time to stand and stare?" So stand and stare they did—at a sunrise or a rainbow, the flaming sumach in the pasture, the blaze of autumn over the hills, the cavorting of young animals in spring, even the senseless clowning of middle-aged cows turned out to clover. And they *made* diversions like the bird station, or a walk in the woods or a visit to an old friend. Something good came from these; a psychologist might call it "human renewal."

Time Is a Pickpocket

Time is a pick-pocket, robbing us of things we can never recover and slipping away while we are blissfully unaware that anything is happening.

"There's a waterfall up in the hills," the old man told the stranger. "Conservation men've been around looking at it. They say there's nothing like it anywhere else in the province. 'Tisn't big like Niagara of course but so high and fierce and white it takes your breath away." No, he had never seen the falls himself. "Lived within ten miles of it all my life," he admitted, "but I never did get to see it. When I was a boy other young-sters had picnics there on the twenty-fourth of May, but I'd rather go to see the parade in town. As a young man I had something better to do than go to a picnic in the woods. But I always meant to see the falls some day—especially when engineers began looking it over and there were pictures in the papers. 'It's a hard place to get to,' one told me. 'The hills are steep and rocky and some places there's no path at all.' That wouldn't have bothered me when I was young but now I have strict orders to keep away from hills . . . I wish I'd seen the falls while I was able. Time has a way of running out on you."

In her widespread clan Cousin Jennie could be counted on in any emergency. Come sickness or trouble or extra work in a house and she would lock her door and go to help. "Jennie has no ties," her relatives said, "and she's so willing." Once she had nursed John's family through scarlet fever with such skill and devotion that years later, when John was drafting a will for his sizeable estate, he left her a small legacy. He wasn't a man to take capital out of his business to make a gift; but with a legacy, when it came due things would be sold anyway. It would come as a surprise to Jennie and he liked to think how pleased she would be that he had remembered her. As time passed he met Jennie occasionally at some relative's funeral and he noticed that she looked a bit poverty-ridden. Fortunately when he was gone she would have something for her old age . . . Jennie never had an old age. She sickened and died in a poor nursing home without knowing anything of her cousin's good intentions.

A mother finds her growing-up daughter withdrawn and evidently troubled about problems of her own. If they could only talk things over! But the girl, dutiful and even affectionate, offers no confidences. And the mother remembers with nostalgia and guilt, an eager, imaginative, little girl, asking the most exasperating questions, chattering about the most impossible things she would do when she grew up, wanting to know about this Prince Charming who was always cropping up in her story books. Her mother might have found a communication then that would have lasted, but she was so busy reminding the girl to do her homework and practise her music and hold her shoulders back that she had no time to listen.

A hard-working couple plan that when the farm is paid for or the new barn built or the children's education financed they will take a holiday or work shorter hours and have more time to be sociable—even with each other. And the years go and some of the capacity for enjoyment and companionship may die from disuse.

Time is a pick-pocket. The wise ones spend themselves as they go.

An Hour to Call Our Own

"The world is too much with us," Wordsworth wrote over a century ago, long before the cult of "togetherness" had made it almost a social offence ever to try to have an occasional hour by ourselves. And the poet points to things we miss in our continuous getting and spending, laying waste our powers—the sight of moonlight on water, the sound of the winds. If this was a cause for concern in Wordsworth's time and in his quiet English lake country, what may it mean for us here and now? Indeed our psychiatrists tell us we may be living too much with others and too little alone with ourselves.

Consciously or unconsciously, most of us seem to need spells of aloneness, especially those who work among people—the teacher, the doctor, the supervisor in business or industry, the mother with a houseful of children. Some of these make an escape to the most secluded places they can find for vacations. Others take less obvious ways. Why did great grandmother, when there was someone to stay with the children, like to go berry-picking in the woods? Of course she needed the berries, but probably she needed a few hours by herself with never a sound to hear but the wind in the trees and the birds calling. Why did a man like to slip away to the back pasture to "salt the cattle" on a Sunday morning? Perhaps the children trailed after him, chattering; but their talk would be far removed from the worries of markets and mortgages—he was still "getting away from things."

I never hear of "salting the cattle" as a country Sabbath custom now; and I know the berry-patch in the woods has pretty well disappeared. It becomes increasingly difficult to find a pretext for being alone. We used to get away for a walk sometimes. Now if someone is seen walking in the country people wonder why he isn't driving a car—and anyone knows you are never more involved with others than you are on the highway. Some women, after a day's housework with whirring appliances, or a meeting that seemed to get nowhere, have found it a rest to "go for the cows" in the evening; but I suppose before long some device will be guiding the cows in by radar. Robert Burns was not the only farmer who did some fairly profound thinking behind the plow; but you can't do this driving a tractor. Country children, left to their own devices, may have a wonderful time setting little water-wheels in creeks, tinkering with mechanical inventions of their own, exploring the woods to see how the wild things live, living out a family drama in a playhouse, reading a book that takes them worlds away. But a child found enjoying himself alone is likely to be herded into a ball game so he won't become anti-social.

There are experiences in a lifetime that most of us will have to go through alone and few have had any preparation for solitude. We may have wanted to get off by ourselves sometimes, but we can't hide away any more—"the world is too much with us." It seems that we will have to find ways of being alone without going away. So a woman, once a musician, may find an hour for herself at the piano in the evening, renewing her soul in the music she loves. A man forced into an inactive life by a heart ailment found comfort in "whittling," carving out of wood little horses so lifelike that now he has a steady market for them and a creative interest to fill his days. And there is the limitless resource of reading—not the continuous escape reading that acts like a drug to deaden all thinking, but the illuminating, stimulating, inspiring books that take us away from our environment only to send us back revitalized, better individuals, better company for the people we live with, knowing that the world is with us and being glad of it.

Second Career for Mother

When Jane Allen was left a widow in her mid-fifties, her friends wondered what she would do, alone as she was, her children married "and herself not too well off," for Jim's heart had given trouble early and they had had to sell their farm about the time they finished educating the children, so they had little time to save anything for themselves. But they had bought a modest little house in town and with painting and planting and Jane's skill indoors, they had made a pleasant, comfortable home. She would be very lonely, her friends agreed—"she and Jim had been so close." And how would she stand it to be idle, an old neighbour wondered, "her that was always doing for others."

The family worried about their mother, too. "Of course you'll sell the house," her daughter Margaret advised her. "It would be too lonely for you here with Dad gone. And there'll always be a home for you with us. The children love you. I'd never trust them with anyone else, but with you there I might even go back to teaching."

"I'd hate to give up my home," Jane told her. "Your father felt I should keep it if I can."

"But how can you?" Margaret argued. "It costs so much to keep up a place."

"I might get a job keeping house," her mother said. "That's

one thing I know how to do and housekeepers are well paid now."

Her daughter was horrified. "We'd never let you go 'working out'!" she said. "Besides, at your age you couldn't stand it."

"At my age I'm not trying any endurance tests," Jane admitted, "but I can do housework as easily as I ever could." She had scarcely seemed to move from her chair as she talked, but with a step or two here and there she had tea and hot toast on the table. Her daughters sometimes said their mother used sleight of hand about the house and they declared she could work circles around either of them.

"If you were keeping house for someone you wouldn't be home anyway," Margaret persisted.

"And I would miss it," Jane said, "but home would be here to come back to. Perhaps I could just help people through emergencies and be at home between times."

But how did one find such emergencies, Jane wondered as the days passed and the outlook bleakened. The trouble, she knew, was not just being alone. All her life people had needed her, depended on her. She had been happy giving herself; proud of her knack of making people comfortable, cheering them up if they were depressed, talking things over with those in trouble. Now the neighbours were sending their children around with a piece of pie for her dinner. She, too, had done this for old women and it was frightening to think she must now be old herself. She found some outlet in babysitting for her daughters, washing the curtains or cleaning the silver while the children slept; but it wasn't enough and all the time her bank account was shrinking.

It was through a chance meeting with a doctor that Jane found the opening she wanted. A neighbour with small children had a sudden flare-up of appendicitis. She called the doctor, then telephoned Jane; and by the time the doctor arrived Jane was there, had administered an ice-pack, fed the children and restored general order in the house. While the mother was in hospital she took over the house and the children, had dinner ready when the man came home and was on hand in the morning before he had to go to work. The doctor told the Visiting Homemakers about her and Jane was asked to join their staff.

So at the age of fifty-five, with her family responsibilities behind her, Jane Allen began her second career. She went into homes where the mother was ill or away in hospital and kept things running smoothly. Children were no problem to her— not even a new baby. If it was a first child she showed the mother how to take care of it. She looked after old people, going in for a few hours a day to cook a good meal and keep the house in shape. Sometimes she took over as full-time house-keeper for a while. Where a woman on relief didn't know how to cook or keep her house clean or use her food cheque wisely, Jane was often sent to teach her—she had a way with people, could give a discouraged woman new pride in herself.

Jane might reasonably have been a little proud of herself, too. She was doing something useful, as anyone could see. The people she helped depended on her. She made friends wher-ever she went. And she was earning the income she needed. Without the formal schooling of most career women, she had a vocation, too.

Bad Company

"I don't think much of some of the friends you're making," Carrie Moore complained to her high school children. "That new boy with the fancy car—"

"But Mom," her daughter protested, "every girl in the class wants to ride in that car. What's wrong about it?"

"Partly that he's tearing around in his car when he should be studying. The more you see of him the harder it's going to be to get your year. And," Carrie turned to her son, "Wasn't he the one who brought the gin to the locker-room after the game?"

"Oh, Mom," the boy said, "how narrow can you get! No one had to drink unless he wanted to. Bill didn't grow up in a hick town and that's how things are done where he came from."

Carrie made some other references—to classroom troublemakers and the pseudo-sophisticates defending the new morality.

"You mean we should be snobs and have nothing to do with anyone who doesn't think just like we do?" the children demanded.

"Of course not. You don't stand aloof from anyone; but bad company is bad company and if you mix with it, some of it is pretty sure to rub off on you."

The children went to school wondering at the strange worries of mothers; and Carrie took up her housework. She had her day so planned that for a good part of it she could listen to the radio while she worked. She often said to her friends that a housewife could give herself quite a liberal education, just listening to the radio, or keeping one eye on television while she cooked or ironed or did the mending; and she recommended some very good programs.

Occasionally Carrie listened to other programs that she did not discuss so freely. She had once been shocked at an underground movie—shocked and rather sickened. Over coffee with a few confidantes she said: "You wouldn't think such a thing would be allowed on the screen." But she went back to that program again and again—"just to see how far such pictures will go," she told herself.

Carrie was not an avid reader and she was too conscientious about her housekeeping to waste a good working day reading a novel—reading was for relaxation in the evening; but occasionally she snatched a half hour with a book she could not read in the evening because the family might see it. To friends who were not averse to such books she might say: "Everyone's talking about it, so I thought I should know what it's all about. But really, I could throw it across the room. What sort of mind the author has, I can't imagine. Still, once you start you have to read on to see what happens. I suppose there *is* an idea in it," she might admit. "Maybe I'm old-fashioned."

There was one young woman among Carrie's friends who sometimes troubled her. "She's the world's worst gossip," Carrie told her mother, "but somehow she builds up my ego."

"Perhaps by tearing down some one else so you feel good by comparison," her mother suggested. "I know the type. They can find something to say to discredit a saint; and if they have no facts to go on they hint at something and leave you wondering in spite of yourself. At first when you listen to them you feel as ashamed as if you'd been on a debauch; the danger is that, like the debauchee, you may find yourself going back for more."

On the day Carrie had checked the children about their questionable friends, her mother dropped in; and at the same time the telephone rang. Carrie's telephone reply was evasive: "Could I call you back? I have company just now . . . No. No. I *do* want to hear."

"That was Madge," she reported to her mother, and immediately wished she had kept this to herself. Madge was the aforesaid scandal dispenser.

Carrie had neglected to turn off the television and her mother was looking at a film on one of the most off-colour themes ever presented through a public medium. "I'm sorry," Carrie said turning the dial. "This is a dreadful picture, but I suppose it's life and we should know about it."

"You wouldn't have been so uncertain about that a while ago," her mother said. "Have you been seeing many of these? I understand the taste grows on some people."

And if this were not enough, Carrie saw that the book she had put down was lying right before her mother's eyes. Trying to be casual, she asked,

"Do you know that book?"

"Certainly I know it," her mother said, "I'm on the library board. You'd be surprised, the stuff we have to send back."

"Isn't that bordering on censorship?" Carrie argued. After all her mother was something of a scholar, broad in her reading and an advocate of personal liberty in most things.

"Not exactly censorship," her mother explained. "We believe any responsible adult should be ready to know and to face whatever there is to know; but we're not willing to be agents for the sort of bias you get in a book like that. It's perverted and downright unhealthy."

Then with a twinkle, but not trying to hide her concern, she said:

"I'm afraid you're keeping rather bad company, Carrie—this book, the movie, some of your friends. Remember when you were a girl, how I used to preach to you about this? It's still risky. It has a way of rubbing off."

Mrs. Tulliver's Travels

The members of Mrs. Tulliver's Women's Institute were great travellers. Scarcely a month passed but someone returned from a tour of the British Isles or Europe or Mexico with an array of pictures taken along the way; and these were shown at a meeting for everyone to see.

Mrs. Tulliver had never gone on a tour herself, but she was keenly interested in the pictures. Indeed, she watched so intently that she almost seemed to be looking *through* them for something more. And always she asked the same question: "Did you get to know the *people* at all?" The travellers explained, of course, that this was impossible. There was no time for it, and anyway the language barrier was a problem. They always urged Mrs. Tulliver to take the trips they had taken. "You'd love it," they said. "You have so many friends among the foreigners living around here, you'd enjoy seeing the part of the world they came from."

It was true that Mrs. Tulliver had made friends of many new Canadians. It was she who had brought the Dutch woman and the woman from Norway to meetings of the Institute, and had persuaded them to tell something about their homelands. A Polish neighbour was too shy to "make a speech," so Mrs. Tulliver, with her friendly understanding, "drew her out" in an interview. The Institute members were delighted; they agreed it was amazing how a feeling could develop for a country they had never seen, just by hearing a woman tell how she had lived there and why she had come to Canada and how she felt about her new country.

An Italian woman, who had been in the neighbourhood for some years and still couldn't speak a word of English, had seldom been seen outside her home, until Mrs. Tulliver asked her son to play his accordion at the Institute's family night and to bring his own family with him. And when the party went into a square dance, the Italians, *mamman* with the rest, joined in with all the warmth and gaiety of their race. Said the school principal who made frequent trips to Europe, "That's the nearest to 'sunny Italy' of anything I've seen in America."

When the Institute program featured a study of the North American Indian, Mrs. Tulliver said: "Couldn't we exchange visits with the Indian Homemakers on the Reserve? They're only fifty miles away but for all we see of each other we might as well be living on separate continents." So the white women visited the Reserve and the Indian women returned the visit; and they learned something about their differing traditions and customs but how truly they were sisters under the skin. To a new Indian friend showing her over the Reserve, Mrs. Tulliver said: "All my life I've been wanting to see more of the world and all the time here was a world I didn't know right at my door, and with my own countrymen."

Clearly Mrs. Tulliver was less interested in geography than in people. Along with other women's clubs, the Institute asked for volunteers to go, one day a week, to the residence school for retarded children, to talk with the children, take them for walks, give them some of the mothering attention the attendants had not time to give. Mrs. Tulliver went, and was terribly moved by the plight of the children—moved and inspired to find ways of her own to make them a little happier and brighter. "I've got to learn more about this," she reported. "I had no idea a school could do so much for such children; nor how much they need our help. It's surely true that half the world doesn't know how the other half lives even if they're in the same parish."

It was the same when the church women made Mrs. Tulliver their representative to help convalescing patients in the mental hospital get back into normal life, and to visit friendless old people in the County Home. No tourist ever entered an unknown country with more sympathetic curiosity or such a desire to get close to the people.

"Even with my own friends," Mrs. Tulliver said, "I'm all the time discovering depths I didn't know were there—ideas we had never talked over before, talents they'd never had a chance to use, maybe a loyalty or kindness in them that I'd never appreciated ... Sure I'd like to travel but, whether I ever do or not, I haven't really begun to explore all the worlds right around me."

The Listeners

It was just a little gathering of friends and someone thought it would be amusing to hide a tape recorder in the room and play the record back to us. Of course there was great hilarity when people heard a reproduction of their own voices for the first time—they had no idea they "sounded like that!" Or that a few people together could produce such an ear-splitting babble. And when an old woman whose hearing was not good demanded "Who's that doing all the talking?" some of us were very much embarrassed. It's so easy to be carried away with the urgency of what we want to say; to step into every opening so fast that the quieter ones never have a chance. We were shocked, too, to find that sometimes what we said wasn't as much worth saying as we had thought it would be. No doubt we had all heard that a good conversationist has to listen as well as talk; but in the chatter of a crowd a listener doesn't count for much except to provide an audience—no one needs his encouragement; there's usually more talk on tap than there's time for. The art of listening makes itself felt in quieter places.

Someone says of a friend: "I wish I could have a talk with Mary"; and if you know Mary you know why people like to talk with her. It's like having a rest and a stimulant all at once. Perhaps she "can hardly wait" to tell you something; but she is just as eager to hear from you. She wants to know what you think about things and she drops a question here and there that sets you thinking more clearly than you had thought before.

Or, someone with a problem, say a student deciding on a vocation or which of two jobs to take, may want to talk it over with someone. He has had professional advice but he still can't make up his mind. Mary isn't qualified to advise him; but she can listen while he thinks out loud, and she may be able to take the picture he gives her and set it before him in a new light, so that out of his own thinking he suddenly knows what he should do.

It may be that we find it good to talk with someone like Mary because the easy give-and-take of it leaves us refreshed and rested, or because her listening, which implies a certain regard, builds up our ego at a time when we need it. (And is there ever a time when we don't?)

People who listen often have a special attraction for children. A stranger comes into a house and a small child eyes him with reserve—perhaps other strangers have frightened him with their bold advances; but this newcomer just says a warm "Hello" and leaves it to the boy to take the next step—that is, he listens. And usually it isn't long until even a very shy little one will sidle up with a book or something to show the man who looks as if he would be friendly but keep his place.

The couples' club in a church wanted to do something for

the old people in their County Home, and they asked the matron what would be most helpful, such as entertainment, craft supplies, books. The matron told them that what the old folk needed most was someone to talk to. Because they told the same stories over and over, no one wanted to listen to them; and they felt more and more rejected, until some of them seldom spoke at all. So the club members arranged a crusade of personal visits—the old-fashioned sort of "visit" where people sit down together and talk. They had old men and women telling about barn-raisings and cooking for threshers, the old church tea-meetings, how pioneer neighbours helped each other through sickness and trouble, how times had changed for better or worse. Minds dying from disuse came to life again, just because someone was there to listen.

Then there is the power of listening in education. A public-spirited lawyer undertook to lead a young men's study group in civics. When the subject was immoralities within the law, the lawyer quoted the law and left it with the class to uncover the immoralities that were getting by without breaking it; and he found that in respecting the unenforceable regulations the young men were often more circumspect than their elders. He found, too, that they brought up points they never would have thought of, if their leader had been a talker instead of a listener.

Good listening is not only a gracious accomplishment; it can be a more powerful dynamic than advice or preaching or argument.

The Happy Warriors

"When a dog runs at you, whistle for him." This advice from the philosopher Thoreau is not to be taken lightly. Thoreau would know what he was talking about. In his wanderings over the New England countryside he must have had many encounters with dogs standing guard at farm gates to scare away tramps. But imagine the confusion or downright embarrassment of a dog charging a suspected enemy and being welcomed with a friendly whistle!

The whistling tactic sometimes works with humans, too. A farmer rouses his neighbours to prevent a motorcycle gang renting a house for a hangout in the neighbourhood. The group's leader telephones that unless the house is made available he will bring out a delegation to "talk things over." That, he thinks, should be warning enough to stop interference. But the farmer says to come right along; his neighbours would like to meet them too. This is something new to the cyclists. They get the idea that the farmers aren't afraid of them, that they may have a strategy of their own; and they stay out of the area.

When a Jewish family escaped from Hitler's Germany and settled on a Canadian farm, the neighbours didn't run out and bark at them; they just sat inside their gates and rumbled in their throats. Anyone from Germany was suspect in wartime. But there were children in the Jewish family and their father couldn't think of having them grow up in the same hostility they had suffered in their own country. So he didn't wait for the Canadians to call. He went to them, told them why he had brought his family to Canada and how they hoped to become a part of it. And the Canadians were as ashamed as a dog setting out to attack a man who wants to be a friend.

Years ago, in a crossroads debating society where the debaters often attacked each other with more venom than logic, we had a debater so debonair and courteous—and incidentally so witty—that it was a joy to hear him. He usually followed an adversary with a compliment—something like: "Ladies and gentlemen, I'm sure you all enjoyed that presentation as much as I did. It's always a treat to hear Bob speak. Of course I feel that tonight he is unfortunate in having to defend a cause entirely unworthy of his good sense and intelligence . . ." The arguments that followed would be clear and studied and delivered with force but unfailing good humour. His friendly approach was even more effective when community problems had to be talked out at a public meeting. In very heated discussions no doubt he was sometimes angry inside but nothing could make him show it; and many a time his sheer good-will made people forget their differences and work together.

Later when our debater went into politics, this spirit and the finesse that went with it, served him well. He was of the breed of Wordsworth's "happy warrior" who,

> If he be called upon to face
> some awful moment to which Heaven has joined
> great issues, good or bad for humankind
> is happy as a lover; and attired
> with sudden brightness, like a man inspired.

There is a "happy warrior's" gallantry in the way some people meet a hard piece of work—work that strains the mind and the heart and the spirit, such as the demands of war to fighting men by nature compassionate. And just now I think of the young school teachers—there must be many of them every year —facing a "blackboard jungle," whether their trouble-makers come from a slum depravity or a "privileged" home. Usually the young teacher keeps his worry to himself, often teaching all night in his sleep but stepping out jauntily in the morning, determined to meet whatever comes, as a teacher should.

In the ordinary affairs of living, people who make no claim to heroism may be artists in meeting hard things with a whistle. A man, through no fault of his own, loses employment in the only work he knows, but he hides his inner panic and in middle life or later tries to learn a new vocation. A mother feels her health failing but steels herself to keep a cheerful presence and hold on till the harvest is in or the school examinations are over. A terminal illness strikes someone in the family and the others keep their grief hidden and make the days as happy as they can for the sick one and each other.

Facing death for ourselves —an experience that comes to all of us but which even our theologians seem to expect us to dread—there are the happy warriors like Robert Browning, who had a zest for life if ever anyone had, but who could say: "Fear

death? ... Let me taste the whole of it, fare like my peers ...
For sudden the worst turns the best ... a peace out of pain,
then a light, then thy breast. O Thou soul of my soul, I shall
clasp thee again, and with God be the rest."

What a tower of strength they are, the happy warriors!

Shells

Their mother had brought the children for an outing at the
beach, and with their little pails they ran along the water's edge
gathering treasures washed up in the night. Almost any shell
seemed worth picking up, but if they found something special
they squealed with delight and sometimes there was an alter-
cation over who had seen it first. When something in deeper
water attracted them they were ready to take risks to get it,
protesting strongly if their mother called them back.

By mid-morning each had quite a collection of shells and
pebbles, and they settled down to building castles in the sand.
After a while they tired of this, too; and the boy said, "I'm
going to play with my boats." He had left the "boats" with his
mother for safe-keeping. "He made them himself," the mother
explained, "and he never seems to tire of them"; and shyly, but
with some pride, he let me see them—an assortment of row-
boats and canoes and a "ship," carved with surprising craftsmanship for a child so young.

The little girl was sleepy but before she curled up on a
blanket she fished out from the towels and swim-suits the most
dilapidated doll I had ever seen. "I want Susan," she said; and
hugging the doll close, she went to sleep. "She never goes to
sleep without Susan," the mother told me. "The poor thing
won't last much longer but Janie won't have a new one."

I saw the family again when they were collecting their para-
phernalia to go home. The boy had carefully packed his boats
in their carton; the little girl had her doll under her arm. "Don't

forget your pails," the mother said, and "Are you taking your shells home?" "No," the children replied without any hesitation, and promptly dumped them on the sand.

The words of an old song came back to me. The singer recalled a day at the seashore in his childhood, gathering shells and throwing them away as others attracted him. Now from the viewpoint of age he soliloquized:

> Ah, thus I've said, at every stage
> By toys our fancy is beguiled.
> We gather shells from youth to age
> And then we leave them like a child.

The experience must be common to most of us—continuously setting our hearts on something, gaining or losing it, only to find later that it didn't matter much after all.

The little girl at the beach would grow into a young woman, no doubt revelling in the gaieties of youth, suffering her share of its common heartaches and elated by her little social triumphs. These soon would pass. She might make a place for herself in the arts or professions or business; or, as a matron, she might be proud of her social standing or her home—each new house finer than the last, until suddenly she might find herself alone and lonely in a place too big for her—wanting only the security of a "rest home."

In a few years the little boy with the boats might be a winner in sports or scholarship, according to his bent; and the cheers or the honours would be sweet while they lasted. But an athlete's career is brief at the best and scholarship is soon forgotten—the world looks for performance, for service. If the man should set his heart on wealth, he might acquire it, as millions have done before him, only to find as the years narrow down, how little money can buy of the things he wants most—health, love, a hopeful forward look.

Or he might give himself to public affairs, serving with integrity and the best abilities he had, winning some elections, losing others, being elated when he had achieved something, but often depressed and disillusioned by political machinations;

so that, whatever the honest satisfactions of his office might be, the glamour would go out of it—more shells to strew on the sand.

But I couldn't forget how the little boy had hung onto his boats—the work of his own creative genius and his careful, tireless whittling. And the little girl had never tired of her doll—symbol perhaps of the human relationships that would come into her life and give it meaning. She might forget the very beauty of a young gallant who had loved and left her, but never the face of her mother or the little brother who had adored her or the homely, gentle presence of the man who had shared her married life for years. Or, from the career that meant so much in its hey-day, the competition, the promotions, the honours would be nothing compared with the memory of a troubled child helped through school, a life saved whole in hospital, fairer or more compassionate ways developed in a firm or factory.

Sure we gather shells and throw them away when their day is over. Sometimes we keep them too long. And sometimes we have the grace to know the things that last, and to treasure them.

The Students

"The value of a really great student to the country is equal to that of half a dozen elevators or a trans-continental railway." When Sir William Osler made this observation, certainly his idea of "a really great student" was not just anyone who goes through a university. A student is someone who *studies*, straining every ability he has to find a deeper truth or a better way.

These great students show up dramatically in the history of medicine. Because they had not only keen minds, but the dedication to work endlessly in their labs or wherever their research took them, babies now rarely die of dysentery or mothers of childbed fever. Whole families of children are not lost through diphtheria, nor promising young people sacrificed to "consumption." No one knows the suffering eased by the Curies' almost fanatical study of radium, or Banting's work with insulin. And some youngster now in school will carry on from where these had to leave off.

Inventors, working perhaps for years on one idea, have taken body breaking work from farms and factories. Now and then a pedagogical genius makes life better for children by discovering a way of teaching no one ever thought of before. And sociologists study and experiment in the most backward of all developments—human relations. There are others, at work in smaller fields, and most of us know some of them personally.

Some years ago in an Ontario community a young man came home from the university to farm. Perhaps his university experience had stimulated him to try the untried; anyway he started testing his cows for milk production—something almost unheard of at that time; he kept accounts of the farm business; got seedlings from the government and reforested his woodlot, started shade trees around the place, even got his friends out to plant the school grounds and the churchyard. The neighbours didn't know what to make of him—"a nice fellow," they told me, "but queer." Soon they saw the wisdom of his ways and adopted them on their own farms. They had a student in their midst and they profited, as many another community has profited from such men.

I think of a teacher who studied her pupils as if each were the only personality of his kind in the world—as of course he was. She made friends of the parents, gave some of them a new appreciation of their own children, persuaded many a father to give his family a chance at the education or vocation they wanted.

There was a "country preacher" in the hills, known as "the highland shepherd," because of the way he watched over his flock. He met them in their fields and farm kitchens, at barn raisings and county fairs as well as in church and at weddings and funerals. There was always a welcome at the manse if they wanted a quiet talk; he came to know them pretty well. And if the light in his study burned far into the night he might not be working on a sermon, but thinking or praying or writing some authority about how to divert young Ian MacLaren's interest from the fast crowd he was taking up with; or what to say to old Mrs. Ross who was depressed and frightened because she had to go to a nursing home; or how to get special help for a child "backward" at school. His predecessor, with the best intentions, had barged into such things with little forethought and had sometimes done more harm than good. The shepherd was studying how to help people without hurting them.

And the minister wasn't the only such student in the hills. He often wondered at the shrewd understanding and inborn tact of a practical nurse who seemed to see her patients whole, as if their health was tied up with their general well-being. When a neighbour was "put away" in a mental hospital, this woman went regularly to visit her. She visited a doctor at the hospital, too, to find how she might help her friend, and what the neighbours could do to make her happy to be back among them when she came home. When a boy was sent to jail for stealing, everyone in the hills felt sorry for his mother but they stayed aloof because they didn't know what to say to her. Then the mother told someone she had been "heartened" by a talk with the nurse and people asked the nurse what she had said to be of such help.

"I thought up every good thing I knew about Jim," she said, "and I talked about these. I didn't condone or lament what he had done; just let her know we all expect him to come back to his real self; that he's one of us and we're standing by. At first I didn't know just what to do, but I studied on it, tried to think how I would feel if it were my boy; and it seemed to work."

She had "studied on it"—another thinker at work in her own little corner.

Needed: A Friend

They were old at the time I knew them, but they had been friends since they came to the West over fifty years ago—three young homesteaders and their wives, opening up a new stretch of prairie farm land. And how they had helped each other! Not only with farm work when help was needed, not only in times of trouble or sickness or childbirth when the women came to their neighbour's house and took over like sisters. Perhaps they helped each other just as much simply by being the good friends they were. In later years when sons took over the farms, the parents retired, each couple to a centre where they could be close to other members of their family; so the old friends did not often see each other; but it was an annual highlight of their lives to get together for a "visit."

"There are no friends like the old friends," they told each other. "They know you for what you are and you know them. You can speak your mind knowing you won't be misunderstood." "It rests me to be with Jane and Tilly," one of the women explained. "We know each other so well we don't have to pretend anything—not even that we feel younger than we are." Or a man might say, "I like to mull things over with the boys." But their "mulling over" did not have much to do with the weighty questions of the times. Mostly they

> Talked of many a vanished scene
> Of what they once had thought and said,
> Of what had been and might have been
> And who was changed and who was dead.

Underlying it all was a warmth, a sense of their own worth in each other's eyes, a give-and-take they never found with the new friends who crossed their paths. Like the little company of country folk assembled for a christening in Hardy's novel, The Three Strangers, "absolute confidence in each other's good opinion begat perfect ease."

Most of us seem to have a need for this sort of companionship. I think of three young men in the days when many a student taught school for a few years to put himself through university. They had schools in the same district and they thought nothing of walking twenty miles on a weekend to meet and talk over their teaching problems, their correspondence courses, their plans for the years ahead. The people in their school sections were friendly enough but only the three young teachers understood and gave each other the encouragement they needed.

And there was the doctor, typical of many who came from the Old Country years ago to take a practice in Northern Ontario, in a mining town with a scattering of farms reaching back into the bush. He was a gifted doctor, skilled and dedicated. No road was too rough, no hour too late for him; but the overwork, the cold winters and primitive living took their toll and his health began to break. To keep going he turned to stimulants till it became a habit. When he was taken to a hospital for his own last illness, he confided to his physician: "The loneliness was the worst—having no one to talk to. Oh there were good people around and they wanted to help, but a doctor, of all people, must not talk too freely to just anyone. If I had only had one real friend for a confidant I could have carried on without a drug."

With the isolated pioneers, the young teachers and the doctor, the need of friends is obvious. What about the busy, swinging men and women, active in careers and causes, pressed by more social interests than they can attend to? Do they ever feel the need of a personal friend who is good for them, who, though he may not always be at hand, is never far away in spirit, like a warm fire within reach when it's needed? We need only ask ourselves if this isn't a need of our own.

We are constantly being urged to cultivate the things that give meaning and beauty and joy to living—to read good books, to listen to good music, to have hobbies to relieve the strain of work or to fill our days if the promised leisure of the future gets to be more than we can handle. But who ever tells us, or when do we see for ourselves, that the surest protection from loneliness or depression or a sickness of the ego is to have and to be a friend?

So, for no reason but our own indifference, our own preoccupation with other interests sometimes we lose the best friends we have. Or as we get older some of them die and we still don't care enough to make a place for others.

The Drifters

When the press or television reminds us of the hippies at loose ends or the old men on skid row, I know the problem is not new. I think of drifters I have known personally, and I wonder if the aimless ways of most of these may have one cause in common. "The child who lives with recognition learns to have a goal," the sociologists tell us; and sometimes we find that men and women not knowing where they are going nor seeming to care much, did not have the recognition they needed at the time they needed it.

There was Melanie, "the odd one of the Gaynor girls," one-time school teachers, now chatelaines in their own homes, active in their communities. Melanie had never married, never had a vocation, and apparently no community interest except a concern that the playground equipment be safe for small children. As a young girl she had never had as many friends as her sisters, probably because she lost faith in herself early and shied away from the crowd.

Even at school Melanie was "different." She would leave a ball game to comfort some frightened little beginner crying in a corner of the playground. At a Sunday school picnic, instead of mixing with girls and boys of her own age, she was likely to be the centre of a hilarious primary group. Her mother scolded her for this; said "You shouldn't be seen so much with children younger than yourself. People will think you're retarded or something."

Melanie was an average student. Some things she learned easily enough, but in eighth-grade mathematics she met a road block. This was serious, because she wanted to be a kindergarten teacher and to be a kindergarten teacher a girl must first pass examinations in geometry and calculus. Melanie failed. Because she wanted desperately to teach small children she tried and failed again. "Then I'll be a nurse and work in a children's hospital," she said; but hospitals wouldn't take a non-graduate, either.

"You'll have to do something," the family told her. "Every girl should have a way of earning a living. What about a business course?"

Melanie became defiant.

"I don't want a business course," she said. "Anyway I'd likely fail at that, too. I'll find my own way."

When she was twenty she left home. She answered advertisements for domestic help with small children; but sometimes she could not accept a mother's ways with children; so she moved about a lot but managed to support herself. When a baby was born to a relative she often came and helped to get it started in a comfortable routine; but it was a thankless service. People wanted her when they needed her; after that they might say, "She's a dear, of course, but rather odd, you know."

It was only when Melanie was getting old that the young mothers who had done some child study began to say: "Aunt Melanie is a wonder—a natural with children. Most of what we've learned from books she has known always. Why didn't someone get her into mothercraft or a nursery school? Or if the family had only seen that she had this gift, and had made her feel it was important she might have found her own way of using it. At least she wouldn't have run away from everything; might have married and had children of her own."

Then there was Uncle William who in his last years tried to eke out a living in a little tinkering shop. The trouble with William in his youth was not that he found mathematics difficult but that he found it too easy, like everything else he set out to learn. He went to grammar school and sailed through geometry that puzzled his teachers. All the men of his family played the violin but William was a virtuoso. He also made violins. He would pick up a toneless instrument in a farmhouse, whittle a new bridge from a cigar box and play "Bonny Doon" with a pathos to bring the family to tears. He took lessons from the best teachers within reach, but found them wanting, so he never made a profession of music.

He was something of a philosopher too and he liked to argue, but because he had no debating opponent of his own calibre, he shocked his friends with his theories of Marxism and atheism. They thought he was "smart but a crack-pot if ever there was one." They also thought he was lazy. There wasn't a job he couldn't turn his hand to, but he never stuck at anything for long. When the family farm was sold he took to the road, found odd jobs as he went along, finally ending up in his little repair shop and playing his violin.

Wasn't William's problem a problem of recognition, too? Unlike Melanie, he had no lack of self-confidence. He must have known his abilities were away above most of those around him; and perhaps that was his trouble. He needed the stimulation of minds equal to or greater than his own, so that he would really put his exceptional powers to work. He needed an interest so compelling that he must channel all his powers in that one direction. Then he might have grown into one of the great men of his time.

In William's day, a little less in Melanie's, it was not easy to find a satisfying, reachable goal for a gifted but limited child, or a challenging, worthwhile goal for a near genius. Education offers more guidance now if we will take it. But someone very close to these exceptional children must first see their gifts and their need.

Adventure in Growing

This was the old man's favourite tale and he liked to repeat it around Christmas time:

"It was the year I'd turned fifteen and almost outgrown a part in the 'Christmas concert'; but, big as we thought we were, none of the boys in my class would miss the Christmas tree, for we always got a copy of *The Boy's Own Annual*. Books were scarce among us and this had everything—adventure, travel, how to make things. It gave us something to read all through the year.

"This night the infant class were singing 'Away in a Manger' when a little girl gave a shriek to raise the roof. Someone was peering in the window beside her and, as it turned out, someone who might easily frighten a child.

"Others saw a movement at the window. 'Prowlers' the superintendent said, and started for the door, the sexton following and picking up the poker from the furnace as he passed. Our school teacher had seen the face at the window too. He was a young fellow and he nipped out past the others. He knew who the 'prowler' was and he wanted to reach him first.

"Soon the superintendent and the sexton came back; then the teacher walked in with a boy such as had never been in that church before—tall, thin, shaggy-haired, ragged, a nervous tic twisting his face into alarming shapes. No wonder the little girl had been terrified. This was Tony, a newcomer to the village. His uncle had a tinker's shop over the hardware store; and that summer he had brought Tony from the city to live with him; had rescued him, we found later, from a motherless home, a drunken father and the hunger and abuse that had made him what he was.

"When Tony came to school there were boys who made life miserable for him; and because some of us stood up for him, I guess he thought he had found friends. Anyway he started waiting at his corner to walk to school with me. I didn't like this. It was one thing to be fair against the school toughs but—

I say it to my shame—I didn't want my prestige to suffer by being known as a friend of Tony's. I cut across lots to avoid him, and I had to do it only once before he caught on. He never put himself in my way again.

"And I could have liked him. In spite of all he had missed he was an interesting fellow. There must have been a streak of brains in his family somewhere; for though his schooling had been so spotty that he was behind in most things, he had read everything he could get his hands on, including old magazines from the village dump.

"Now here he was, suddenly brought into the bright lights of our church basement with a crowd of people he had never seen before. I expected to see him bolt, but the minister came to shake hands with him; then the teacher beckoned me to come back stage. He said:

" 'Will you keep an eye on Tony—try to make him feel at home?' I felt quite important being trusted with this. 'Should I go and sit with him?' I offered, pleased with myself to have thought of such a heroic gesture.

" 'Fine,' the teacher said. 'He shouldn't be left alone and I have to help with the tree. And *there* we *are* in trouble. We haven't a thing to give him.'

"It hit me like a blow in the stomach, the thought of what I should do. There was just one thing for me to say and it was so hard to say it that it came out in a sort of croak: 'He could have my book.'

" 'You would really do that!' the teacher said; and the way he looked at me made me stand a good inch taller. I began to get into the spirit of the thing. I suggested we make up a parcel of hymn books to put under the tree for me so no one would ask any questions. Later, when Tony's name was called and he was so overcome he couldn't get to his feet I took the book down to him. And I accepted my parcel of hymn-books with a grace that may have been a little overdone.

"When we got home my mother wanted to see my book. I suppose she couldn't understand why I hadn't opened it yet.

And when I explained what had happened she was downright angry.

"'I can't understand the teacher at all,' she scolded. 'He knows you care more about that book than anything else you get for Christmas. The idea of letting a child do a thing like that just because he's good-hearted enough to offer!'

"My father didn't agree. He said 'Maybe the teacher sees signs that Jim isn't such a child any more, that he doesn't have to be spared everything that isn't easy. You're growing up, son —that was a thing a *man* might do.' And the second time that night I felt myself growing.

"I never tried to keep out of Tony's way after that. In fact we got to be very good friends. I even went to the room over the hardware shop sometimes to read his book. With the sort of teacher we had and the boys being more friendly, he made some progress at school; and after a while his nerves got back to normal. He grew into quite a good citizen, carried on his uncle's business and was one of us. I've often thought how different it might have been if the men had chased him away from the church that night.

"But that young teacher thought of everything. I've sometimes wondered," the old man added, half to himself, "if he wasn't thinking of me, too—seeing me caught in my comfortable, self-centred, play-it-safe little world and giving me a chance to break out of it."

A Lesson in Giving

The wise men who found the Christ Child and presented their gold and frankincense and myrrh, left a lesson in giving for all time.

The gold must have been a soundly practical gift—the Holy Family would need it in their wanderings in Egypt. It may have been used to buy something as mundane as a saw and hammer, so that Joseph could support his family as an itinerant carpenter. Unquestionably, gold or its equivalent is a wise man's gift *to those who need it.*

Providing for material needs, not just at Christmas time but all the time, is often more costly than we know. There is the man with a family to support, who stays with a job he dislikes or a boss he hates, when he would quit in a minute if he had only himself to think of; the construction labourer knowing well the hazard of the high scaffold on a windy day, the weak-walled tunnel in the underground, who keeps his worry to himself because of the household of children depending on him. We think of a young teacher in a "blackboard jungle" school, close to a breakdown but lasting out the year because without her salary her brother could not go to college. And the mothers who work harder than most wage-earners to have a clean house and good meals and fresh clothes for the family; who, if they feel tired or ill, keep it hidden until after the harvest rush or school examinations. And the family who "share their loaves," doing without new clothes or movies to buy food for a hungry child across the world.

Frankincense and myrrh stand for another kind of giving—giving that puts a fragrance in the air, that says "You are some-one very special." It seems that anyone who gives frankincense and myrrh gives something of himself—the most precious, most potent of all gifts, and the gift of which we are generally most niggardly.

The little boy who comes home crying because he couldn't do his "rithmetic," or the boys called him "Cow's tail" because he was last in every race, doesn't just want his mother to give him "a piece." He wants her to sit down and let him tell her about it. His ways have fallen in pleasant places if his mother is one of those women who can restore a man's ego when he has almost lost faith in himself. We have all seen such a woman giving herself to her family. She will leave an ironing half done to pick up a crying baby and hold it for a while. She is not irritated by a little runabout trailing her at her work. She finds time to read to small children, to tell them stories and to listen to them—perhaps most important of all, to listen. Whether she gives encouragement or restraint or just wholehearted attention, both friends and family know the comfort of her caring.

There is the gift of companionship. Almost anyone is ready to invite a lonely neighbour in for Christmas dinner. But occasionally we find someone who *understands* loneliness—all sorts of loneliness, all through the year, and even with the family, and who finds a way to fill the emptiness and set things right.

And there is the gift of appreciating people and letting them know. Children thrive on this and are blighted without it. Inarticulate young people in love, and husbands and wives need it from each other; but how dumb and blundering we can be! It's a sort of giving most of us haven't learned yet.

A Time for Open Hearts

"I have always thought of Christmas . . . as the only time in the long calendar of the year when men and women seem by one consent to open their shut-up hearts"—Scrooge's Nephew in A Christmas Carol.

Scrooge's nephew, buoyant, generous soul that he was, may have been overly optimistic about shut-up hearts opening at Christmas time. People may be too tired from shopping and making ready for a feast to go the second mile of the eager heart. But some will.

The high school alumni Christmas club was sending groceries to its usual list of families in need; and a student checking deliveries pushed a box back on the counter and said to the principal:

"I don't think we should send anything to the Hills, this year. Jim's home and he might be hurt."

Jim's friend remembered a Christmas eve four years ago when he had been all excited about the box he had to deliver to the Hills. Another high school boy had been with him; and as they came to the house they could hear Sam Hill, roaring drunk, cursing and throwing furniture about. Jim had come to the door in an agony of embarrassment, disgraced by his father, ashamed that his family should be on a charity list. Soon after that Sam had left home for good and Jim, at sixteen, had quit school to help his mother support the family. He had not been a very good student—too many worries at home, perhaps; but he was strong and quick and steady and able to do a man's work in the mines a thousand miles away. With his help the children were fed and clothed and their modest little home took on a certain dignity and comfort. Now Jim was home for Christmas—a man, proud to be providing for his own, but still walking in the shadows of an old disgrace.

"Jim doesn't need groceries," his friend was saying. "He needs something for his ego such as an invitation to the reunion dance. He can't come as a graduate but he sure could qualify on his record of achievement. We've got to make him see this."

The principal could not quite see how he could frame a citation for what Jim had done; but he was sure his friend could attend to that. Youngsters today had minds of their own and this one seemed also to have a heart.

Nancy Brown was almost a professional at planning parties for the Old People's Home. This Christmas holiday almost every organization in town was entertaining the old people and Nancy had a hand in most of it.

Then she discovered something: that what most old people want is not a party, but a personal friend—someone who will sit and "visit" with them as their old friends used to do. There was the old man whose poor hearing missed most of what was said in a crowd—he needed someone to talk to him alone; and the old woman without a single relative or friend to come to see her or even write a letter. She confided to Nancy that it would be like old times if some busy woman would only let her drop in and give a hand with the mending or sit with the baby while its mother did her shopping. Nancy Brown enjoyed being a social hostess—she did it well. But she had the rarer gift of an understanding heart. She decided to let someone else take over the organizing; she would concentrate on being a friend.

The Mercers, a proud family, had a problem not uncommon these days. Their son in university had made a close friend of a girl of another race. His mother told herself that she did not want to interfere, that the best thing to do in a case like this was to ignore it, which she did so completely that the boy stopped trying to talk about the girl at all; and there were long silences in the house—in modern terms, "communications broke down." Finally the boy's wise old grandmother could stand it no longer. She said to her daughter:

"You're afraid Ted will marry this girl. I suppose he might— from what I hear he could do worse. More likely, though, years from now he'll remember her as a lovely oriental girl among other girls it was good to know. But he'll never forget that there was a time when his mother didn't want to be his con- fidante, didn't care how he felt about something that meant a lot to him. I wonder," the old woman went on, "why we are so ready to give our children anything under the sun except ourselves."

"Not you!" her daughter said. "You were always on hand knowing just what we needed." She remembered the comfort- ing: "I know how you feel. It's hard but you can handle it"; or the heartening, "You did that well. I'm proud of you"; or the reassuring "I agree with you. You did right to stand up for what you believed even if everyone voted against you."

The open-hearted act on a warm impulse before it has time to cool; they are up and at it when they suddenly feel they must see an old friend they have neglected for years; must write to thank someone for a kindness done long ago and only now fully appreciated; must go all out to get to know the folk around them—the newcomers, the afflicted or unfortunate or withdrawn or embittered, the charming, and gifted, and friendly, the members of their own family—especially the family.

THE FAMILY

A Place in the Family

The film was a documentary on family life in different parts of the world. A mother in India gave her baby a bath with about as much speed and as little tenderness as she might put into washing a rubber doll. In France, children coming home from school received little attention from a father and mother completely engrossed in the baby. So far as the school-age children were concerned, there was no carefree chatter, nor any warm communication with their parents.

When the film moved to Canada I expected something better, and it *was* better, but still lacking something. The family appeared first in a supermarket—father, mother and children loading a grocery cart. They got into a modern car and drove through miles of wheatfields to a ranch type farm house. Parcels were carried into the kitchen—a very modern kitchen of course; foods were stored in the deep freeze and the endless cupboards; then the woman went to work—click, click, click with never a move wasted. Gadgets whirred, frying-pan hissed, tea-kettle whistled, and in three minutes flat there was a meal on the table and the family "fell to with gusto." You don't dawdle over a meal in the movies—production time is costly. I don't remember that there was any conversation. After the small ones had gone to bed the father went about the room picking up a litter of mechanical toys. The day was over.

It seemed a poor picture of family life in our country, but perhaps it is not as far out as we may think. Our hours are so pre-empted by our work, our clubs (every member having his own), our bowling or curling or hockey or badminton if we're sports-minded, or our favourite television programs if we sit at home, that there isn't much time for association as a family.

A man who is proud of his children and of the good home he can give them, is afraid they may be missing something. He remembers his own childhood in the depression years. Times were hard; but in his family the children didn't ask for things they couldn't have. "We knew just how hard up we were," the man said. "We all had our bits of work around the farm and were rather proud to have a part in seeing there was food on hand, sometimes taking a sack of potatoes or a cut of meat to someone who had nothing. It was a great feeling for a teenager to be something of a partner in the family business.

"We had most of our entertainment at home, too," he went on. "We couldn't buy toys, but our mother could contrive a rag doll or a baseball from odds and ends around the house; and for the little ones Dad could whittle a spinning-top out of a spool. He made us a checkerboard, men and all. And kites! On a windy day in spring it was nothing to see the whole family take off across the fields flying paper kites.

"We couldn't afford to go to the movies but there was a library in the village—no funds for new books of course, so we got to know the classics pretty well. The whole family read and we talked about what we read. It may not have been very literary talk but it certainly wasn't dull. One's ideas seemed to spark another's.

"And how we laughed together! Looking back now, I think maybe our parents encouraged this because they didn't know how much worse the times might get, and they wanted us to have whatever fun we could as we went along. When I see people pushing their kids to learn this and learn that, get ahead whatever else they do so they can make a lot of money, never taking into account that they're children only once, I know we were lucky.

"We had music of a sort, too. Sitting around the fire in the evening someone would strike up a song and everyone would join in. None of us ever aimed at being a musician but we liked to sing, as long as we could sing together.

"Best of all we had time to talk—and to listen to each other. I suppose today this would be called 'communicating.' The little ones, if they felt lonesome, would go straight to our father or mother to be picked up and held for a few minutes and they were never disappointed. When we came home from school our mother was there to hear about our day. Often an older brother or sister would give us a word of advice or encouragement. It was all in the family. We had a grandfather who was a born story-teller and when he came to visit, we kids never let him out of our sight. He liked to talk about what he called 'the clan.' So, as the psychologists say, 'the social base of our family broadened.' We felt we had a solid place in the world.

"I know the life we had wouldn't do for today," the man admitted. "Our children have to move at a faster pace; have to be trained for harder things than we had to do. But I wonder if they wouldn't face the hard things more easily if they had, back of them, the place we had in the family."

Love with Insight

A young women's church guild had been helping the Elizabeth Fry Society with clothes for girls released from prison; and as they met the girls at the hostel, the women wanted to do more for them. So someone suggested they invite them, "in a body so they wouldn't feel strange," to a Christmas party in the church. Another member demurred. She said, "I'm wondering if a girl at a party like that might feel she was still just a prison number, not a woman in her own right like the rest of us." This member felt that what a girl with a prison experience needed most was a personal friend. She herself was getting acquainted with a former delinquent and persuading her to go back to school. Paul's advice to the Philippians to have love *with insight* is practical and timeless.

Such insight may be found at its best in a family. A mother entertaining some friends one night was startled to see a little boy in pyjamas steal down the stairs, then, seeing the visitors, sit down on a step and cry. She went to see what was the matter. Outside in the warm spring night the frogs in the pond were in full chorus; and the little boy was thinking of his frogs in a tub in the yard. "I can't hear my frogs singing and I think someone has taken them," he cried. "I came down to look." His mother didn't send him back to bed. She got a flashlight and took him out to see that his frogs were all right. One of her friends, perhaps trying to make an excuse for the child's behaviour, said, "He may be a great naturalist some day." "I don't know," the mother said. "I only know he's a little boy now and for some reason this was important to him."

With such insight, parents give children freedom to live their own lives; and the guidance that comes of growing up in an atmosphere of love with intelligence and vision. A few have the insight to know what children need of them, like the taxi-driver who told me he had two little girls; one was "pretty as a picture," the other was "homely"; but, he said, "You know I kind of lean towards *her*." I doubt if he had ever studied child psychology, but somehow he had a special concern to help the little girl who would always be outshone by her sister.

Love with insight is quick to build up the ego of the "unsuccessful," the discouraged, to make them aware of their worth. A matron in an old people's home says that the best therapy for old age depression is not entertainment or hobbies, but the visits of sons and daughters and friends who come to see the old folk, not out of a sense of duty but because they like to talk things over with them, even to ask their advice occasionally, or just to be with them.

Sometimes young people surprise us with their forethought. After a high school graduation dance some girls thought of sending a newspaper report to a classmate in a tuberculosis sanitarium. "I don't think we should send the report," her best friend said, "it would only make her more homesick. I'll write and tell her a little about it." "You won't tell her that Tim brought Ginny!" the others warned. "Of course not. She liked Tim herself. I'll tell about so many saying how they missed her—and Tim was one of them." It's a great gift, this insight into the feelings of other people.

A Baby Is Heavy

The child psychologist, visiting her married sister, was ready to "take the children off their mother's hands" as much as she could. They were delightful children, so well loved and well cared for that they presented few of the problems familiar to a psychologist; and their aunt accepted them eagerly when, freshly groomed and fed, their mother handed them over and gratefully went ahead with her other work—the daily washing, the tidying of the house, the preparation of the day's meals with a thought for the special needs of a two- and a four-year-old, the formula for the baby. Her work load was heavy but with the added care of each child her speed had accelerated.

The children's aunt was not idle either. The two-year-old liked her and climbed on and off her lap with the persistence of an athlete in training. The baby, with a vigour out of all proportion to her size, bounced in her arms and made it clear that she liked this much better than lying down. The older boy brought story books to be read, toys to demonstrate. It was all very sociable and lively. But somehow the two-year-old got crowded out of things. He banged pot-lids like cymbals to get attention and when his brother tried to take them from him, his screams started the baby crying too. It was more than a psychologist could cope with, but when their mother came everyone quieted. She listened to the four-year-old's story but knowing how the middle one sometimes suffered from two directions she took him on her lap for a while. Her sister said, "You're a better psychologist than I am," but the mother explained, "You get to know your own."

It was time to feed the baby then and the aunt, handing her over, said, as if she had just discovered something, "You know, a baby is *heavy*." Her sister chuckled. "And more so at the end of the day," she said. So she knew what it was to be tired.

A baby *is* heavy, especially when there are three of them, heavy not just in the weight a mother lifts and carries through the day, in the feeding and dressing—"the buttonin' and un-buttonin'" an old nurse called it, the washing and sewing and mending, but in watching over their health and their habits, the shrewd, gentle guiding of their growth in mind and body.

"The children look like their father but they talk just like you," their aunt told her sister. "I suppose they hear my talk more than anyone else's," the mother reasoned. "Our neigh-bour's family have acquired quite a dialect from the sitter who stays with them while their mother is at work."

The psychologist was on familiar ground here—she had seen children taking on the personalities of their attendants. Her sister was giving hers the best of herself when they needed it most. She had been a professional musician; some day she might go back to this; in the meantime she sang in her own house and her children sang with her. And she was there, lov-ing them, teaching them, giving them security for the years ahead. It meant security for her husband, too, having the family so cared for. He had wondered if she might find it boring to stay at home with children. She didn't find it boring; it gave scope for every skill she had and the rewards were past measuring. But it wasn't easy. A baby is heavy.

The Carefree Years

The school bus stopped at the gate and the children came
running to the house. Even the little girls had their arms full
of homework books and the boy, twelve years old, had a small
library strapped to his back. Their mother was waiting for
them, ready to give them "a piece" and to hear about their
day—but briefly; more and more, where the children were concerned, she had to keep an eye on the clock.

Before the little girls had swallowed their buns she had the
evening mapped out for them: "If you'll get right at your
piano practice, Mary, I'll help Anne with her homework; then
she can practise while I help you. After supper you can both
work at your Brownie project."

Tim ate his piece standing, eager to get out to the barn.
He liked working with the men and his calf would be waiting
for him, though he wouldn't have much time with it. "Come in
as soon as you finish your chores," his mother told him, "and
we'll get a start at your math before supper. You have a Scout
meeting but it should be over by nine, so you'll have a while
to study after that."

That night when the children had gone to bed, the girls
cross and tearful because they were too tired to get their
stitches right, Tim after he had fallen asleep over his books,
their father said:

"I don't think it was ever intended that kids should live like
this. They haven't an hour of the day to call their own, no time
to play, no time to enjoy their home. Everyone's pushing them
to *learn* something."

"But they have to be pushed," their mother argued. "There's
so much expected of them. And a lot of what they do is playing, in a way."

"Not really," the man said. "Tim stays after school for hockey
practice two nights a week. That may be a ball for the star
players but not for the others, with the coach telling them to
win or else. He plays in the orchestra and likes it. It's good for

him. But it's one more thing he has to make time for. And of course he wouldn't give up the calf club. Thank heaven the leader has a boy of his own in the club and he knows how driven the youngsters are; so they do as much as they can in school holidays."

At a parent-teacher meeting the mother heard that a dancing teacher in town was opening Saturday classes for children; and she decided that by getting the family up a little earlier she could manage to bring the girls to the classes. She even thought dancing classes might help Tim to acquire the social poise so important in the education of modern youth. But Tim's father put his foot down. "Any boy Tim's age would hate it," he said. "When the time comes for him to go to dances he'll learn to dance—he'll have a reason for it then."

More and more the father became uneasy about the regimentation of his family.

"Whoever said children have a carefree time?" he wanted to know. "It seems ours know nothing but care. Sure, youngsters need lessons to learn and chores to do; but they need some time to do what they want to. They need a chance to be children."

There was Tim, going around like an automaton, trying to do what was expected of him, not getting much excitement out of anything, haunted by the fear of failing in examinations. In a year or two there would be the added fear of failing socially, not being like everyone else. "The kid's got to have a chance to rise above it," the father stormed to himself; "to grow in his own direction." Tim loved horses. "I'll get him a horse," the father decided. "Then whatever comes, with a horse to ride and chum with I'll know he's having some good times as he goes along."

The man had often been amused watching little girls "playing house," unconsciously imitating their elders and doing the most original things on their own. His daughters always seemed to be doing what someone else had planned for them. It wasn't fair. So he built them a playhouse with some small furniture and dishes for tea parties. They caught on like magic. They bustled about like house-proud women and giggled like little girls. They wouldn't be cheated out of their childhood entirely.

The One Who Didn't Pass

At the village post-office a little assembly waited for the morning papers that would bring the results of the high school examinations. The papers came and as each local name was discovered the youngsters became a bit hysterical; even the men in the gathering raised a few cheers. Never had the school made such a record. In a class of fifteen, fourteen had passed. The boy who had failed was not in the gathering—he had received his verdict by mail the night before. His friends thought of him and said it was "too bad he hadn't made it"; then they dashed out to spread their own good news.

The school principal stayed to read the report again. He was proud of his graduates; he rather felt they should have some public recognition, a commencement banquet perhaps. But a younger teacher got into his car and drove out into the country to see the boy who didn't pass.

The lad was even more shaken than the teacher had expected. Seeing a visitor crossing the field he brushed his sleeve across his eyes before he climbed down from the tractor. He was ashamed of his failure and he couldn't waken from the nightmare that his hope of being an engineer, the thing he wanted more than anything else in the world, was gone forever.

"But you'll try again," the teacher encouraged him. "Next year you'll get through." "I don't know," the boy said. "Dad thinks maybe I'm not cut out for university. I guess he's right."

The teacher had come at the right time. He called the father into consultation. He pointed out that the failure had been in subjects not related to engineering; that where engineering talents were involved the marks were good. Because he cared as he did, the young teacher was able to put heart into the boy and to convert the father into letting him go back to school.

Surely there is something wrong in the custom of pouring out our commendation when people have had a success that is a reward in itself, and ignoring those who have failed and need, desperately, to have their confidence restored.

When the thing we call disgrace strikes a family, often we hesitate to go near—not because we don't care but because we don't know what to say.

A young man who meant a great deal to his family, had been drinking at a party and on the way home he drove his car into another car, killing both the couple in the other car and himself. Of course indignation ran high in the community. Some called the accident "cold-blooded murder." Added to this, neighbours who called stammered out only an awkward sympathy—they seldom mentioned the boy at all, and it seemed to his parents that no one now believed any good of their son.

But one understanding soul spoke out so others could hear. She said: "He was the thoughtfulest boy I ever knew. Who else would have carried the little polio cripple home from school night after night? Old Mr. Dean says Jim seemed to know when he needed a hand to lift a hayrack or something and he'd be across the fields like a deer." Others caught the spirit and added their praise of the boy whose heart had been in the right place even if he was irresponsible sometimes. They could see that the family needed this more than they would have needed congratulations if Jim had won a medal for life-saving.

Status Symbols

Seeing a child as an asset or a liability to the public image of the family was in practice long before we ever heard of "status symbols." The patriarch who ordered a disgraced son or daugh-

ter never to "darken his doors again" was telling the world
--though he may not have known it--that he cared more for
his own prestige than he cared for his child. Such harshness
may be uncommon today, but in some families children are
still status symbols.

The Teacher had lived all her life in one town. For fifty years
she had taught the town's children—first the beginners, later
the high school grades; and she knew the homes they came
from. She knew the little eight- and ten-year-olds who came to
school with sick stomachs because they had examinations to
write and their mothers expected them to do well. She knew
parents who were not satisfied unless their "bright" child
headed the class; and she was familiar with the plight of the
child staggering under the shame of being what is called "slow
at school." This last angered the Teacher more because she
had seen so many of these children when they were given a
chance at schooling that was right for them, turn up later
among the most respected, useful members of the community.

As a counsellor on vocations the Teacher came to know
fathers and mothers who had already chosen their children's
vocations to fit the family pattern; the industrialist who was
determined to have his son come into the business, when the
boy's heart was in social work; the fifth-generation farmer who
felt that the dynasty would fall apart if his son did not take
over the family farm, while the boy wanted (of all things!) to
be a commercial artist. And there was the high school orator
with a genius for teaching, whose mother would settle for
nothing but a law course and a career in politics.

Fathers and mothers who believed that the best thing a girl
could do for herself or her family was to make a good marriage,
sometimes blocked a brilliant daughter's way to a profession
like medicine, and were terribly embarrassed if a girl of the
family got herself involved in public causes, however right
they might be.

Boys who had neither the desire nor the physique to play
rugby or hockey were sometimes badgered to get into the game

by a father who had either played himself and wanted his son to keep up the tradition or who had never had a chance at sports and looked for the vicarious experience through his son. By way of the same self-fulfilment, a mother from a family where girls always had a lot of beaux, or one who had been deprived of social life in her youth, sometimes urged her daughter to grow up too fast, to date too early, to sell her birthright of personal development for a mess of passing popularity.

In these days when youth, at least in theory, is all for social democracy, the snobbery of a status-seeking family can be sadly disillusioning to a son or daughter. A woman who was an active church worker seemed rather proud when her son, still a student but a candidate for the ministry, started giving voluntary help in a downtown mission. But when he found he could be of more use if he transferred his membership to this congregation in the slums, his mother was horrified. If she had been questioned, of course, she would have said she was thinking only of her son's good, but he knew that his mother was one of those who want their children to make friends only on their own economic and cultural level. If they can do a little climbing—well, that won't do the family image any harm. . . . It seems a mean load to put upon children.

The Talking Family

Most of us have heard the tribute to the "reading mother": "Richer than I you can never be—I had a mother who read to me." On the same plane, H. C. Mason writes of the talking father: "I praise whatever gods there be—I had a father who talked to me." This father seems to have been well-versed in history and folk-tales, for his son says that while he "held the brown cow's tail and the milk rose foaming in the pail," he listened to stories of Bruce and Wallace and Saint Joan and Robin Hood. His father talked from memory, too: "While we went with rope and grain to fetch the horses up the lane, he told me how he'd heard it read when *he* was little, 'Lincoln's dead.'"

Perhaps it was not important that the boy learned history from his father—he could get that from other sources; but it was important that they talked, for from the companionable tone of the record we are sure these talks would be two-way conversations. No doubt the boy talked as much as he listened, so his father would know pretty well what was going on in his mind and in his life among his friends; and these would be talked over, too. Whatever wisdom the man had about a boy's problems would find a natural outlet in the talking that had become a habit with them.

A talking grandparent can be a treasure to a youngster. Who else knows the old tales that give us a pride in our good ancestors, something to live up to, and a warning about the weak traits that run in the family strain? And who else has time to sit and talk with a child at the time he is ready to listen to this? Grandparents, too, sometimes know how important it is for a child to enjoy his childhood. With their own children they may have been so busy seeing that they did their homework and held their shoulders back and remembered their manners that they didn't think much about whether they were happy or not. Now they know that a child's talk with an older person who cares about him can be relaxing and amusing and enlightening to both.

We hear a good deal about the significance of family table talk. We are told that public opinion is formed around the dinner-tables of the nation. Such education is certainly commendable—we could do with more of it; but it isn't the greatest good to come from a talking family. Take a look at the Cratchits in *A Christmas Carol*. Settled around the fire after their Christmas dinner, they talk about Tiny Tim and their hopes for his health, about the prospect of a better job for Peter, about Martha's work as a milliner's apprentice and the titled customers who come to the shop. Dickens says: "There was nothing of high mark in this. They were not a handsome family; they were not well dressed. But they were happy, grateful, pleased with one another and contented with the time." And they talked as many another family have talked, about each other's achievements and problems and what the future might bring. It isn't hard to imagine the comfort and confidence they gave each other.

If the Cratchits had had more leisure time together, it is possible Bob might have drawn them out to express their thoughts on such things as the meaning of Christmas and what society should do for children like Tiny Tim; and through this their thinking would have deepened and they would have learned to say what they thought—another heritage some children bring from their homes.

Some of us remember a special brother or sister who was always ready to listen to us, even when we talked about some far-out dream, something we wanted to do that seemed impossible at the time, but that came to pass later partly through their encouragement; or the troubled younger one who wanted a confidant. What a help it was in these times to belong to a family who could talk to each other!

It's a strange thing about some married people, that the longer they live together the less they have to say to each other. This is something quite different from the restful silence between kindred souls who don't need words to express what they feel. It seems to grow out of taking services for granted, feeling foolish about paying a compliment, withholding praise when it is due or, worse yet, when we need it to restore our faith in ourselves. There is the silence of hurt feelings that goes on and on until all sorts of misunderstandings develop. Other couples aren't afraid to say "I'm proud of you." "What would I ever do without you!" If a grievance comes along they have built such a bank of devotion and admiration and trust that a sharp little quarrel isn't going to wreck it, so they talk it out. They may have learned that in either good times or bad, talking never conveys exactly what we mean, but it helps; and finesse grows with practice.

Little Pitchers

"Little pitchers have big ears." The old warning must have come from someone's discovery that children have an amazing capacity to take in what goes on around them. When what they hear is good, or even simply enlightening, it's a happy thought that they may remember it all their lives, which, I suppose is why most people make a serious business of trying to have their children exposed to influences likely to leave impressions worth having—the imprints of a good home and whatever "cultural" experiences are available.

I wonder if they ever think of what rubs off from the comers and goers who visit the house. In my day children kept in the background when we had company, but our eyes and ears didn't miss much; and I still enjoy the philosophy, the colour and humour, the glimpses into how other people lived and felt, that came to us by way of our visitors.

There was the minister, scholarly, something of a mystic, but as concerned with this world as he was with the next. He could talk with men and women on questions of the times, drawing out their thinking, too. In college he had been something of an athlete, so he had a common ground with the boys on sports. And he liked music. Because I had a sister studying singing, I overheard more about the oratorios from the minister than I have heard from anyone else since. I am glad I was allowed to stay around and listen.

We had "characters" in our neighbourhood. One of these who called occasionally was considered "odd" just because he was a dreamer with a keen mind. He was always on the verge of discovering perpetual motion. He knew the medicinal plants of the woods and gathered ginseng roots as a vocation. He was "well read" on world affairs and discussed them freely; but he had ideas of his own ahead of his time, so some people believed he was a little mentally unbalanced. But how his talk fascinated us children! Already I have seen some of his prophecies fulfilled; and I am gradually learning never to dismiss a dreamer lightly.

In our settlement it was a custom for neighbours to drop in on one another for casual visits, and the children of the hosts were seldom out of earshot. The chat of the women was comfortable to hear but not very exciting. It was different when the "wits" of the neighbourhood called. Then the grown-ups would scarcely be settled around the fire before bits of repartee began flying back and forth and the place would rock with laughter. Perhaps I didn't know then how clever some of the talk was, but I remember a lot of it and I know now that it was good. Besides, I began to see what a good time friends could have together with one mind sparking another and everyone enjoying it.

There was never much talk of politics except when the visitors and my father adhered to the same party—then they could let themselves go; but I don't recall any stimulating discussions. Men were keenly partisan in those days and I imagine political arguments were saved for the blacksmith shop where they could call each other names if they wanted to.

Occasionally we had visits from people who had grown up in an area so far from a school that many of them could not read or write; but they had a culture of their own. They knew a great many songs of the Kentucky folk variety, and one woman could reel off one after another almost endlessly, keeping time as she rocked in the kitchen rocking chair. One evening a man brought a visiting relative to entertain us with step-dancing. Most of these people could step-dance but the visiting cousin was a virtuoso. His repertoire was tremendous and as he announced each number, "double shuffle," various versions of "buck and wing" and others, and went into the dance with the dedication of an artist, my horizons broadened. I have since seen professional dancers performing this old art, and it had significance for me only because I knew what it meant in an actual folk way.

On a Canadian farm fifty and more years ago we had few

contacts with other parts of the world. But a man who had come from Germany years before to get away from the military regime there, brought his young family and settled on a farm near us. They were delightful people and very musical, so we had many a good evening with them. And when the man talked about his homeland I would leave even the singing to listen. (I wonder if children today are as fortunate in getting close to people of the many ethnic groups settling among us.)

In the book *Memory Hold the Door*, some of Lord Tweedsmuir's precious recollections are of seeking out the retired sea-captains in his father's congregation to hear their stories, and of talking with the old shepherds on his grandfather's farm. From the sea-captains he "became aware of the largeness of the globe." And of the shepherds, he says: "I have striven to acquire some tincture of their philosophy of life, a creed at once mirthful and grave, stalwart and merciful."

We learn so much by listening!

Conflict of the Generations

It may be that psychologists make too much of what they call the "conflict of the generations." A mother of a grown family says: "Our 'conflicts' amounted to nothing more serious than a difference of opinion about dress styles and haircuts, which I though it wise to ignore. If you're continually nagging children about things that don't really matter, they're not likely to be much impressed by your views in a more serious disagreement."

Perhaps some of these deadlocks are to be expected. Just because of the difference in years and what they teach or how they mislead us, the most well-meaning son or daughter and father or mother may come to an impasse where neither logic nor persuasion has any effect whatever.

In Marjorie Kinnan Rawling's novel, *The Yearling*, we have

a story that might be an allegory of all honest rebellion of youth and the anguish of frustrated, responsible parents. The Baxter family, Penny Baxter, Ma Baxter and Jody, live on a poor farm. Jody is an only child and often lonely, but he has one of the best fathers a boy ever had. Penny teaches him about hunting, the life of the woods and a sound philosophy of living. He also wants him to have time to play while he is still a boy. Jody's mother won't let him have a pet; but when he rescues a fawn after its mother has been shot, his father lets him keep it. They are friends from the first, and surely a boy never had such a playmate. Together they run wild over the bush trails, "beyond the sink hole, past the magnolia tree, under the live oaks."

But the deer grows fast, and soon he is a yearling. When a fence is built to keep him in a corral he sails over it like a bird. He eats the Baxters' crops and, worse yet, the crops of their neighbours. He will have to be destroyed. Penny explains this to Jody as gently as he can. He, personally, would see that death was made quick and easy but he is sick now and cannot get from his bed. He tells Jody that he will have to do what has to be done himself.

The boy is outraged. To kill the deer would be like murdering his best friend and he tells his father he can't do it. His father understands; but the deer has to go. Penny sends Jody to his room; the boy hears a shot and rushes out to see that his mother, whose aim is not good, has fired the gun and the deer is horribly wounded. In a hysteria of rage and grief he screams at his parents that he hates them and hopes never to see them again. Then he shoots his pet to put it out of its misery; and he runs away from home.

Is any family with a teenage son or daughter immune from such a conflict? Suppose your sixteen-year-old daughter becomes infatuated with a boy who is not only bad company for her but unsafe company; and as her father or mother you can't allow her to go out with him. The girl feels you are heartless and narrow and snobbish; that the boy has his bad reputation just because everyone is against him. Perhaps she tells you that as soon as she can she will leave home and never come back. And you wonder why all your love and pride in her, the security that gave her such confidence, the good times she has had at home—how all these could come to nothing.

But this isn't the end. How did things work out with Jody Baxter? He found a boat and tried to row across the river to a place from where he could "go to sea"; but the current carried him steadily downstream. After a day or two a steamer picked him up and put him off at the port nearest home. By this time he was thoroughly homesick. The thought came to him that his father's sickness might be worse. What if he should die? Maybe with no crops left they had moved away. And he found himself running down the road towards home, crying, "Pa, wait for me!"

At home he was welcomed with a relief and warmth that almost unmanned him. This was where he belonged, where he wanted to be. He would plant another crop; he would get a doctor for his father; and Penny said: "You went away a boy; you've come back a man." Later in his own bed where the cornhusk mattress felt so good to his aching bones, he planned the work he would do the next day. Once he wakened from a dream—"down beyond the sink hole, past the magnolia tree, under the live oaks, a boy and a yearling ran side by side and were gone forever."

Because of what Penny Baxter had built up in his son in the early years, because of the good life Jody had known at home, he could not have stayed away. In spite of the hurt he had suffered he was pretty sure to turn out the way he did. Wouldn't any of us be drawn back to a place where we had felt loved and wanted and responsible and important and happy? It's an old, old rule for child guidance; and the Irish have a simpler way of putting it: "You get in your best licks while they're little."

In Praise of Fathers

"Let us now praise famous men," said the Preacher; and the men he named for praise were "such as did bear rule in their kingdoms, men renowned for their power . . . leaders of the people . . . by their knowledge of learning, . . . wise and eloquent in their instructions, such as found out musical tunes and recited verses in writing, rich men . . . living peaceably in their habitation." Perhaps we might interpret these to mean statesmen and men of affairs, philosophers and scholars, authors and artists, orators, musicians, actors and the men of means who live comfortably and "peaceably" or we might say with a good will duly recorded in endowments and charities.

"All these were honoured in their generations and were the glory of their times," the Preacher continues. "There be of them that have left a name behind them." And so they should. It is right for us to remember the able, brilliant ones whose gifts have been a blessing to their time.

But this is not the whole story. The canticle adds: "And some there be which have no memorial; who had perished as though they had never been . . . But these were merciful men: whose righteousness hath not been forgotten. With their seed shall continually remain a good inheritance: their children are within the covenant . . . Their seed standeth fast for their sakes." These men were righteous, kindly and self-effacing. They had no memorial except the children they fathered and guided so well that they are "within the covenant . . . standing fast for their fathers' sakes."

Isn't this something we have seen over and over again? How often are our great men and women the sons and daughters of famous fathers or mothers? The famous man or woman is usually so involved in responsibilities or ambitions that there is little time left for children. Dickens who could wring a reader's heart with the troubles of Oliver Twist or David Copperfield or Little Nell, was a notorious failure as a father. Men who give themselves to public affairs sometimes pay a heavy price in the instability of their children. A woman who is a popular socialite or a brilliant crusader or a clever actress or a successful career woman may have a daughter who grows into a mousey, frustrated woman because she has always been overshadowed by her mother.

This need not happen, of course. Lillian Gilbreth, of the story *Cheaper by the Dozen,* a construction engineer and mother of twelve children, was a career woman if ever there was one. She had to be to support her family after her husband died. She was also a genius as a mother. Her children adored her and even when she had to run her household by remote control, communications were so good and the family climate so warm and sunny that the youngsters took responsibility and thrived on it. But Lillian Gilbreth gave herself wholly to two concerns—her work and her children; she had no interest in building a public image. A man in the same position might find it difficult to get time off for his family.

Happily we have men whose own destinies may be obscure enough but who see to it that their children have a chance to make the most of theirs. Go to a family reunion and you may find a half dozen men and women known the country over for their achievements in one field or another, and somewhere in the background a quiet man who had worked hard to send them to school, encouraged them when they needed it and had done his best to set their feet in straight paths. You will see many men and women, unknown beyond their own communities but good citizens wherever they are, carrying on in the traditions of their fathers who were "merciful" men and "righteous."

And at the same reunion almost certainly there will be many a young father with his children close to him, as the children of most young fathers are today, secure and relaxed in his presence and growing in his image. If the Preacher could have foreseen this trend he might have added another verse to his song.

A Place for Grandparents

"A broad social base in the family gives a child a feeling of security," said the psychologist. "It can help to have grandparents around."

A woman listening thought of her little boy who was shy and nervous. The only grandparents he had lived miles away in the country. Anyway she had always believed that grandparents made things difficult for children, spoiling them when they were little, criticizing their ways as they grew up. So she was not entirely happy when her husband's father asked them to take over the home farm and live in part of the big house. She felt that to live under the same roof with her husband's parents, even in well separated apartments, would not be good for any of them, especially for a child sensitive to any conflict among his elders. But her husband had always looked forward to going back to the farm.

Away from the city streets and playgrounds the boy was thrown on the resources of his family for company; but this turned out to be no problem at all. He liked to "visit" his grandmother. They had great talks, or rather, she let him talk and she felt no responsibility to check his facts or his English as his mother would have done. She had never studied psychology but after raising several children she knew how to put a troubled one at ease. She told him stories, mostly about things that had happened in her own time and to the family for years before that; and he astonished his father by what he knew of the family history.

"I think you've told him more than you ever told us," the father said to the grandmother.

"I didn't have time to sit down and talk when my own were children," she explained.

The boy's grandfather was always fixing something around the place: mending a fence, re-hanging a sagging gate, planting a tree; and always the boy was right there, watching. His grandfather got him a few small tools so he could "help" (and learn). And always they talked—about the lambs and the calves and the growing things. Together they stole through the bushes to look into a bird's nest or explored the fence-rows for blackberries. If the boy came home from school when his mother was out driving the tractor, his grandmother was there to take him in, give him "a piece" and hear about his day. It was a good life for a boy.

He was ten years old when his grandmother died, stricken without warning by a heart attack. It was a hard blow for a youngster but his people noticed how he forgot himself to comfort his grandfather. Perhaps, understanding something of the frailty of age, he wanted to share his young vitality.

The old man, almost deranged by his loss, was rather difficult. He declared he would not be a burden to anyone; he would move into the County Home; and he did. But he hated it; hated the rules; almost cried when the matron said he should not wear his old sweater. Even if his wife had made it, its day was done. "Like mine, I suppose," he snapped.

Hearing this, the boy was outraged and he was no longer afraid of combat for a cause. "They're not going to push grandpa around," he said, "I'm going right now to bring him back." His mother said, "I'll go with you." She was sure they could make the grandfather see how much they all needed him—especially the boy.

The Closed Circle

They were such a "close" family, people said. Even when the children were grown up their mother often told her friends how sorry she felt for people whose children were always away in the evening—hers would rather be at home "in the family circle." She believed she could take some credit for this; they had always played games together, they had their own little orchestra though they were not serious musicians. Occasionally one of the boys would suggest inviting in a friend with his violin or clarinet; but she had discouraged this. "I think music holds a family together," she said. "You lose something when you bring in outsiders. And I think most children today don't have enough home life." With this last thought, at least, most of her friends agreed.

The Avery children had begun to feel their family ties early. No babies were ever more loved and sheltered; and as there were four of them they had a little social centre right at home and everything a child could want to play with. They took care of their things, too, and no child from outside was ever allowed to touch them. Mrs. Avery dreaded the day when the oldest would have to start school, and when the time was only a summer vacation away she confided her worry to a neighbour who had the same problem before her.

"You can't help worrying a little," the neighbour admitted, "but I'd feel worse if there was something wrong with Jimmy so he couldn't go to school; and I'm doing what I can to prepare him for it. Like your little boy, Jimmy's the oldest of ours so he'll have no big brother to help him and he might be frightened. So this summer I'm having the neighbours in whenever I can, so he'll learn to play with other children and, I hope, like it."

"You have some pretty rough children among your neighbours," Mrs. Avery reminded her. "It breaks my heart to see a child from a home where he's been protected from everything hard and ugly, step out into what he'll meet at school."

"I know," Jimmy's mother agreed, "but it seems that a home has to be a launching-pad as well as a haven. I'm sure the birds find it easier to shelter their fledgelings in the nest than to teach them to use their wings."

The Averys had belonged to the same church for generations so it came as a shock when one of the boys, an inquiring youth, announced that he wanted to join another church. The denomination was not very different from his own; but it had some special appeal for him, inspired an interest he had not felt before. Indeed his mother had been a little troubled by his growing indifference. She told him she had nothing against the church he favoured—she would be quite content to worship there herself; but if he were to leave the home church it would be an awful blow to the family. There was such a feeling of "oneness" about worshiping together in the family pew. So the boy stayed in the family's church until his interest in religion petered out altogether.

As the Avery girls grew up, young men began calling at the house and asking for dates. Mrs. Avery was rather pleased with this and the young men were entertained most graciously in the bosom of the family. "Home is the place where young people should meet their friends," their mother said. She was more reticent about dates away from home. And none of the girls' admirers was quite what she wanted as a son-in-law. She would warn her daughters, "Remember, we'd be taking him into the family." She often said that of course she wanted her children to marry, "but not for years yet."

Neither did she want their work to take them away from home. She was very proud of an engineer brother who had made a name for himself building bridges in South America; but when he offered her son a chance to work with him, she couldn't think of having the boy go so far away and take the sort of risks his uncle had taken.

One of the girls had an ambition to be a doctor, but her mother laughed that down. "You're not the type," she argued. "You're a homebody if ever I knew one. The time will come when you'll want a home of your own. Till then, what would we ever do without you here?"

Mrs. Avery didn't worry about the future. As she grew older she felt that she was blessed above most women, in having her family circle still unbroken. It never occurred to her that her children might want more than the circle that was complete for her, but not for them. She did not see that the close little circle, cosy as it was, had robbed one of the comfort of a religious faith, two of the fulfilment of a chosen career, and had delayed all of them having families of their own. She had entirely forgotten that a woman had once said to her, "A home has to be a launching-pad as well as a haven."

Working Mothers

It was a museum display of butter moulds—little wooden contrivances that farm women once used to shape butter into "prints," topped with a design of wheat or acorns or something else according to the impression in the wooden mould.

The first moulds were round, but these were soon followed by a brick shape measuring out an exact pound of butter and with no decoration other than a possible line or two, as women began to make quantities of butter for market and wanted it in a convenient shape to wrap in parchment and pack in a basket.

I looked for some time at the out-dated tools, their handles worn and hollowed by hands that were strong and capable and often deadly tired. And I thought of what the farm mother's "butter and egg money" had meant to the well-being of her family some generations ago. It provided groceries and clothing and sometimes a new parlour carpet or a chair or two. When children were ready for high school their mother might insist on having another cow, so there would be funds to pay their way. Talk about "working mothers"! "Married women in gainful employment"! A woman who made butter to sell was an income-earner if ever there was one; and what her hard work did for her children is now generally appreciated.

"But," we say, "the woman who helped with her butter and eggs was always at home when her children came from school. She was there to give them 'a piece' and hear about their day." Actually there wasn't much time for conversation when the children came from school; they had their chores to do and she had cows to milk and supper to cook. But the children could feel that their mother was near by, and she knew where they were, and they would all be under their roof together when the day ended.

Today when the children of a working mother come home from school she isn't there; but they know when to expect her. If she is a good mother they know she has them on her mind and will be with them as soon as she can. Like the children of fifty years ago they have their chores to do and their sense of responsibility may be just as serious. This family, too, when the day is over feel good about being together in their own house.

But the two working mothers have this in common: they haven't enough time to spend with their children; so if they are good mothers they will try to make the *quality* of their family life make up for what it lacks in actual hours with their children. They will try to have laughter and good talk around their tables. They will have an alert eye for the individual who needs them. Does John want someone to listen to his "impossible" plans? Does Mary need assurance that her plain young wispiness is already turning into willowy grace?

The dual role of the working mother was never easy. It demands wise planning and great self-giving. But some of its results have been amazingly good.

"They're Never at Home"

"How can children get a feeling for family life, or any culture in it, if they're never at home?" The question comes up at conferences on the family; it troubles parents who want their children to have the experience of a good home life but who have to compete with scouts, cubs, brownies, guides, 4-H, church groups, high school extra-curricular activities and, later, all the social interests that youth finds for itself.

A mother knows it is important for her children to have friends outside the family, but she may look back to a time when young people brought their friends into their homes. Children were invited to a neighbour's for a Saturday afternoon. With a hill for sleigh-riding or an orchard to play in and a friendly mother to welcome them in for supper, it was an occasion to remember. The farm kitchen was a popular place for a neighbourhood dance—more hospitable and friendly than the village hall. Young people went to one another's homes on a Sunday evening. (Where else was there to go?) They sang around the piano and usually the older people sang with them. Anyway they never thought of getting out of the house because the young people had friends in, as parents sometimes do now.

Courting was done mostly in a girl's home parlour, not in a car or a movie theatre—the parlour was a room then, not part of an open suite with broad vistas from one area to another. The home, in addition to being the setting for an individual's personal life, was the centre of his social life, more than the school or the church or any community group.

The old way was not entirely good. Acquaintances were limited, and there were no "co-ed" programs to stretch the mind or stimulate the imagination. Still, these projects that bring young people together take them away from their families; and some parents complain, "Our company isn't enough for them any more. They want to be with their friends."

Then why not do what our grandmothers did—open our homes so that children can enjoy their friends and their families at the same time? A twelve-year-old may not find a family dinner very exciting, but he would if his best friend were there. A teenage girl who likes to loiter at the drugstore for a coke with her friends after Sunday school, might find it more fun to bring the crowd in for a pass-around supper occasionally and to take the hostessing responsibilities herself. A man who provides a baseball diamond or a skating pond for his boys and their friends is likely to have them around home most of the time.

One reason why young people of another generation stayed close to the family was that they were all bound up in the work of the farm and the home; they had a common interest even if it was not always a satisfying one. The home is no longer a centre of industry but it can be a centre of special interests. We have the reading family and the musical family. A mother who got an electric organ, partly for "company" in her evenings alone, soon found a son or daughter always at the piano to play duets with her. Having a pony waiting for him may bring a boy home early, even from a ball game.

And perhaps nothing draws a family so close as interest in a common cause—helping each other through school, crusading for some community good. These know that "Love is not gazing at each other, but looking outward together in the same direction."

The Law and the Family

"Police records show our greatest number of delinquents to be between the ages of sixteen and twenty," the policewoman said, "but no one suddenly becomes a delinquent at sixteen. The trouble starts long before that." And she assured us that it is no kindness to a child to let him get away with even the slightest venture into breaking the law.

Police personnel, it seems, have little patience with parents who don't know where their children are or what they are doing in their free hours and who don't seem to care much. If their teenager is caught shop-lifting or drinking, they can't believe it. If a policeman asks if they didn't know anything about the company the boy kept, if they had never helped him to get into healthier interests, they explain how busy they are. Where the offence is very serious, such as joining a gang to terrorize the community, the juvenile court may remember that when the boy, at ten years old, was brought in for throwing stones through the window of an old man's shack, his people were ready to laugh it off as "the prank of a high-spirited boy." Told that some fathers, if their boys broke a window, would see that they apologized and used their spending money to repair the damage, the lenient mother thought this might give the boy a "guilt complex."

The officer didn't know exactly what was meant by a "guilt complex," but he knew boys; and he said: "If he has it in him, by the time he's paid his debt and made friends with the old man in the shack, he'll be so pleased with himself he'll be looking around for a chance to do someone else a good turn. There's many a fine man today blesses the parents that never let him get away with any bit of meanness. The law might well bless them too; they save the courts a lot of trouble."

And mightn't we all well bless the homes that—more than schools or churches or youth programs—keep our people not only law-abiding but going the second mile, meeting the unenforceable regulations cheerfully because that's the way they like to live.

We hear of parents who don't know where their teenagers are at night. Some youngsters are *at home* because they are encouraged to meet their friends there. Many a farm has a ball field or a tennis court, a pond that doubles as swimming-pool and skating rink, and a hill alive with skiers on a winter night. We are told that fathers and mothers haven't the least idea of what goes on in a child's mind or his life with his friends; but if there's someone on hand to listen when he comes home from school, usually he can't blurt it out fast enough. There are mothers and fathers too—who are such good listeners that their children hold back nothing. So if they're headed in a wrong direction they can be diverted before much harm is done.

Law courts know well the men who try to get ahead by cutting a corner here and there, until they find themselves in real trouble, their guilt exposed, their careers wrecked. Is it possible their homes might have saved them? We think of a Scottish mother whose boy, proud of his business acumen, showed her a jackknife he had come by in a trade. "It's worth half a dozen of the one I gave for it," he boasted. But his mother said: "Then you'll be taking it back to the boy and telling him. A hundred years your father's people have been in business and never took a cent for value they didn't give. Sharp deals just don't go in this family."

When we are shocked and sickened by the more sordid things that get into the courts—violence, sex degradation, brutality to children, murder, we thank God for the homes that nurture gentle people, homes where the strong bear the burdens of the weak, where children learn early to respect the rights of others in the house, where the highest praise is not for heading the class or scoring a goal, but for going out of the way to make things better for someone else, homes where there is always a place by the fire for outsiders who are destitute or lonely or handicapped or troubled, and children learn that it is their business to help, not to hurt.

There may be no specific sex education in these homes but children know that their parents love them and love each other, and as they grow up they are likely to bear out the prediction of K. Pelky, social worker with unmarried parents, that "If the word sex was left out of training in schools and homes and the general problem of living with each other in love and kindness, justice and responsibility stressed, sex would take care of itself." Here again the good family is the friend of the law.

Challenge of Adversity

The town was proud of its high school. Board members, teachers and parents generally felt that youth should be concerned with the public affairs of its time; and their students seemed to have taken on a responsibility beyond their years. They not only spoke out against war and poverty and prejudice; they tried to do something practical, from the little "candy stripers" helping in the hospital and the teenagers watching over retarded children on the playground, to the hockey players having games with the young men on the Indian Reserve.

Teachers thought of what all this might be doing for the students themselves. Were they growing in compassion and a social concern, in self-confidence and courage? Were they in earnest about wanting an education that would fit them to set right the wrongs that worried them?

There was one girl who had no part in these interests. After school Marian Orr went straight home because she was needed there. Marian was perhaps the most serious girl in the school; and certainly no one could say she didn't care about people. "She's always the first to know if anyone's in trouble," a friend said of her, "and she thinks of things to do without making any fuss. It's too bad no one can help her with *her* problem."

Marian's problem was pretty well known in the small town. Her father was an alcoholic and when he was drinking he made life a very hell for his family—his gentle, hard-working wife and his children—Marian and two little boys. Marian, a sensitive seventeen-year-old, more than once had come to school marked from a beating when she had interfered to protect her brother, the frail little one who was beginning to have a nervous tic and a stammer.

When Marian failed in her matriculation exams the teachers were thoroughly distressed about it. Now, they said, she might drop out of school altogether, and what future would there be for her? They would like to tell Tom Orr just what he was doing, making her life such a misery that she couldn't keep her mind on her school work. It was maddening, the teachers said, to see such an out-going girl, a promising leader among young people, tied down with the cares of her family. If only they could get her away from home. If she could be kept in school till she graduated, maybe sometime later she would find a way of making something of herself. So when it was rumoured that an aunt in another town wanted Marian to stay with her and go to school, a teacher felt she must have a talk with the girl.

"But I couldn't leave home now," Marian said. "As long as I'm here I can ease things for the others. When Dad has his spells it's really awful, but I think I'm made a little tougher than Mom. I'm not really afraid any more—just sort of sick at my stomach. The main thing is to keep cool. Sometimes a pot of coffee helps to sober him. Generally I can get the boys off to bed before he comes home so they don't even see him drunk. That's the important thing—to protect the children.

"You may wonder why we don't leave Dad," the girl went on, "but it isn't as simple as that. He does support the home in a way, though Mom works too; and when he isn't drinking he has his good points. Breaking up a family is a serious thing to do," she said with the conviction of one who has had advice on it. "—unless, of course, living with Dad should really hurt Timmy. I asked the doctor about that and he said the best thing to do just now is to hang on, and he'd talk to Dad about Tim." Then, with something like a twinkle in her eye, she added: "But I'm getting older all the time. Maybe before long I'll have a talk with Dad myself. And if it has to done, I'll go to the family court," she declared, "but I don't think I'll have to."

She would be coming back to repeat the year at school; and when the teacher suggested that if she had to live in the same turmoil she might fail again, she said:

"I won't fail this time. I've got too much at stake. You see, since I've been taking Timmy to the doctor, I've decided I've just got to go to university and learn to work with disturbed children. University is expensive, but I'll find a way." And the determination, dedication, or whatever force possessed her, left no doubt that she would.

The teacher was rather stunned. The most "underprivileged" girl in the class, a girl so handicapped by her environment that she could take no part in the school's social movements, would probably do more social good than any of the others.

It's strange, the teacher reasoned with herself, that with all we know about the blights from an unhappy childhood, we forget the great ones in history who were great partly because of the hardships of their youth—the young Booker T. Washingtons, so eager for an education that they literally or otherwise scrubbed floors to pay for it; the Barnardo Home men and women who had so felt a child's need of love that they more than made it up to their own children; the doctor giving his life to stamping out some sickness because his mother had died of it when he was a boy.

Perhaps, the teacher thought, schools should teach more than they do, that we are the results, not only of the influences around us, but of standing up to them.

The Irresponsibles

They came out of church ahead of me after collecting their children from the nursery—a toddler riding high on his tall, young father's shoulder, an infant of a few weeks asleep in its mother's arms as she stepped along, the mini-skirt of her smart, spring outfit swinging jauntily.

"So young to have the responsibility of children!" some older people may have thought as they watched them. But obviously the responsibility wasn't weighing heavily on the young parents. They seemed to be enjoying things—the spring morning, the walk to the parking lot, the church they had left, their children and each other; and perhaps they were meeting their responsibilities better than some older fathers and mothers. While some of these might be still asleep in their beds this Sunday morning, leaving their children to go their own ways, the young parents must have been up early to get everyone fed and dressed in time for church. Possibly it never occurred to them that it would be easier to stay at home. Their church meant something special to them and they wanted their children to have this too.

And since they found it no burden to have the children with them, no doubt they would all share other interests—story-telling and books and games and chores about the house (where for a while the children would be "something between a hindrance and a help"), and friends, maybe at a later date even differences of opinion that could be mutually appreciated because they had understood each other pretty well all along.

From my window I have a view of the back of a tenement house. One apartment opens directly on a little yard with never a blade of grass growing; and this winter a very young couple with a baby moved in. As soon as the snow was off the ground the boy was out there in the evenings with rake and spade, making things tidy, planting something along the fence. On sunny Saturday afternoons the girl comes out with the baby to watch him work. And sometimes—times when she is busy, I suppose—the young father brings the baby and sits on the doorstep in the sun. He doesn't know he has an audience and now and then he interrupts their efforts at conversation to hold the baby close and kiss the top of its head.

Of course the boy is too young to be the head of a family. He hasn't even a good way of earning a living yet; but he's doing his best. And whatever material things his baby may miss, it already knows what it is to be loved—which is more than some children ever know, even though they may live in what we call a "beautiful home."

Not long ago a law student and his young wife were tenants in the apartment building where I live. A few months before he was called to the bar their baby was born. The young man has a brilliant mind and some of our conversations were rather over my head. Now his first thought was, "Have you seen our baby lately? My, he's cute." And he was—a handsome, healthy little boy filled with the joy of living. Then I met them all at the door one evening, the baby cheerful as ever, the parents obviously distressed. The girl said, "We're taking him to the doctor for his first shots and we feel like traitors."

But they were seeing that he got his protective shots and were suffering them with him. Not much irresponsibility there!

Such "happenings" lift the spirits in a time when we are shocked at the not infrequent court cases of brutality to children by their own parents—usually by a young father, mentally immature, emotionally unstable, unable to cope with the responsibilities of a family; when we hear of mothers abandoning their children to some makeshift care while they go out to work—not so much because they need the income as because they want more *things,* or because they are bored by children and housework.

I asked a doctor about the outlook for children in the face of all we hear about new trends in family life and the role of women.

"It's good," he said. "Women are learning that a young child needs its mother, or a substitute almost as good, such as a grandmother. It needs both her care *and her company.* And a nice girl, smart enough for a career, doesn't sacrifice a child to it. If she goes to work when her children are a little older she tries to make it up to them when she is at home. Fathers get into the act, too, and there's no telling how much it means to a youngster to have two parents instead of one."

The doctor had something to say about the need of good day-care for children as accessible as the public school to any family. To counteract the violence of the times he recommended the study of human relations from kindergarten to college, with a special concern for gentleness in the family. "Even families who already get along pretty well could do with more of this," he said.

Only Son

He was the only son of his mother and she was a widow; and she never let him forget it. He would always remember that when his father died she had held him close, crying over and over to her friends, "He's all I've got." It was a claim he learned to live with.

But life with his mother was pleasant. She looked well to his creature comforts, talked with him, entertained his friends —firmly rejecting those she found undesirable. Always she was his closest companion herself.

Now she was an old woman in an old people's Home—a nice Home but an institution nonetheless, complaining to a visitor that it was a mistake for a mother to live solely for her children.

"No mother and son could have been closer than Ted and I," she said. "As a little boy he was never hard to manage. We had our little differences, like the choice between hockey and piano lessons; but in the end I could always make him see that I knew best.

"In high school he got the idea he wanted to be an engineer, travel all over the world building bridges or something. I just couldn't have taken that—Ted on one side of the world and me on the other. But right up till he was ready for university, nothing but engineering would do him, even though I had wangled a good job for him with our local brokers. It was quite a battle, and he might have won if I hadn't come down with a heart attack or nerves or something. Anyway, Ted was sure his stubbornness had brought it on so he gave in.

"Life was lovely after that. As I said before, we were very close. If he had an evening out I was always awake when he came home to hear about it. Often we went out together. He was always ready to be my escort and I was so proud of him.

"Of course he had dates. Girls were crazy about him. And I expected him to marry—but not just any girl, and not until he was old enough to know what he was doing. Unfortunately, it seemed that every girl who attracted him—they were the nice girls of the town, too— had some flaw. A boy's mother can see these where the boy himself wouldn't; and because Ted confided in me so freely I could warn him before he got too involved. So the time came when all the girls around Ted's age were married and it seemed the beautiful life we had might go on forever.

"Then, without warning, the brokers asked Ted to take charge of their Western office. I was desperate. I argued that he didn't need the extra salary; he would have everything of mine when I was gone; but the president, rather rudely I thought, said it would be good for Ted to move—he was getting into a rut.

"I can't tell you how lonely I was with Ted gone; but somehow I felt we'd be together again some day, until—it still hurts to think of it—he wrote that he was engaged to be married. The girl was a school teacher almost as old as himself, and she would continue teaching. And I had always wanted marriage for Ted to be a *romantic* affair! I didn't go to the wedding— I couldn't face it; but I went to visit them later.

"They were living in an apartment but were saving to buy a house. (Ted had always said that when he married he would build a house with an apartment in it for me.) I should have preferred to have *them* living with *me*; still, I would have tried to fit in, and under the same roof I could have done things to give Ted the kind of home I knew he would like and which he certainly wasn't getting from *her*.

"Both working, they were always in a rush—rushing to get away in the morning, rushing to get dinner at night, and often just delicatessen fare. The worst of it was Ted didn't seem to care; so to remind him of old times, one morning I said: 'Tonight I'm going to cook dinner. Don't worry about supplies. You're to be my guests.'

"I went out and bought a roast—something they had time for only on Sundays. I made a lemon pie; I set the table with the good silver and candles; and when they came home I was the gracious hostess, waiting. They entered into the spirit of it like children. And how Ted enjoyed his dinner! *She* praised it too, but Ted went overboard. 'We never get a roast like this,' he said, and 'I haven't tasted such a pie since you made the last one. You make me homesick.'

" 'If Ellie had more time . . .' I said, trying to apologize for her. 'Oh, I know, I know,' said Ted. 'Ellie's carrying an awful load. We've nearly enough for the down payment on a house now, and I couldn't have done it alone. A woman doesn't have it easy these days, being both wife and worker.'

"I was really angry. After all I had done for Ted, how could he think Ellie's going to work was such a sacrifice? I said, 'Sometimes I wonder if it's worth it, this grasping for two incomes'; and I set out to tell them just what he was missing. Perhaps I said more than I meant to. I think he was rather stunned. Anyway, all he said was 'You can't have everything.'

"We hadn't been paying much attention to Ellie. Now she stood up and her eyes were blazing. She said, 'I'm sorry you've been missing so much Ted.' Then she flung herself out of the house, for all the world like a bride going home to mother. Ted started after her but I stopped him. I said 'If you run after her now you'll be doing it the rest of your life.' But of course he did. A wife has a terrible power.

"When I had a good chance to sell my home I moved in here," the old woman ended her story. "I never thought Ted would let me go to a Home, but he seemed to think it was a good idea; said he'd come to see me often, and so he does. Ellie comes too. But they never say anything more about buying a home with a place in it for me. I suppose I'll never know why."

To Educate a Mother

In a radio seminar students and teachers discussed the high school curriculum. Among the young people there were the radical and the conservative, the practical and the visionary, the committed protestors and the brilliantly original and far-seeing. It was one of the good youth programs of the times—a cross-section of uncensored teenagers speaking with a sincerity and sometimes a shrewdness that must have amazed their elders.

When the audience got into the arguments, a girl complained that the high school course was not giving her what she needed for her future as a mother. She would like to limit her study to home economics, to be free of such non-essentials as geography and history and especially mathematics. She said, "How will knowing that x plus y equals z help me in raising my family?"

It was good to find a girl taking so seriously her responsibility as a future mother; but I wanted desperately to tell her that she was missing something. I wanted to tell her about another girl and what her education meant to her family.

This girl, Sarah Jane, according to reports was very attractive, caught up in the joy of living but more serious than most people knew; and she had a thirst for learning unusual in a girl at that time, almost a hundred years ago. Higher education for women was not easily available then; but she went to grammar school and a "ladies' finishing school"; and some of her teachers must have been pedagogical marvels—otherwise she would never have been exposed to the tremendous range of knowledge her children found in her later.

Somewhere along the way she picked up other bits of education. From an itinerant teacher of designing she learned to draft dress patterns and to sew. (When she was fourteen a neighbour's baby died and, as the custom was, women came and sewed all night to make "mourning" clothes for the family.

Sarah Jane took charge of the cutting and fitting, drafting the patterns herself.)

Oh, and there was a singing school in the village winter evenings, where she learned to "sing by note." She read everything within reach and because this included the Bible, *Pilgrim's Progress*, Dickens and Scott and the classic poets, all her life she had a feeling for good literature which naturally rubbed off a bit on her family.

When Sarah Jane was married at eighteen she went from a home of comparative affluence to a precarious living on a raw, new farm. She had a large family and she worked hard, not only to create such comfort as she could for them, but to help provide their living—these were the days when many farm children were clothed and sent to school on their mother's "butter and egg" money.

But what she did for her children in a material way wasn't a patch to the other things she gave them. From the time they were babies they heard singing in the house and they, too, sang before they could talk. Later, if they came from Sunday School with a piece of music to learn for the Christmas concert, she could sing it at sight and teach them any part. When they went to school she was with them every step of the way, giving a little light where it was needed, making learning important. If someone encountered a French or Latin phrase in a book she could translate it, usually adding a word about the limitation of knowing only one language.

To Sarah Jane a tricky problem in mathematics was as intriguing as a cryptic puzzle to a puzzle fan. She would lead a youngster to try to solve it for himself, making a game of it. If it was really difficult she worked at it herself till she found the answer. (This happened once with a problem a daughter brought home, unsolved, from a school teachers' convention.)

Any science she had picked up at school must have been very elementary but it had started a continuing curiosity. When she took a stick of wood from the woodbox she might stop to show her children an interesting bit of lichen on the bark. Often she had them out of the house at night to see the beauty of the stars. They learned early to wonder at the world around them. . . . Because Sarah Jane was a reader, books found their way into the house and everyone read them. They had conversation in the family too. With a mother like this and a brood of children inheriting or acquiring some of her interests, there were minor debates and seminars around the supper table. Sarah Jane's education certainly had not included economics or politics, but perhaps a mind disciplined to grapple with mathematics develops some power to see through public affairs. Anyway she liked to talk them over and the children liked this too.

Sarah Jane's life was not easy. Troubles that might have embittered or broken another woman left her serene and sweet. "She had such resources in herself," a daughter said. "Sometimes when she was encouraging us to study she quoted: 'My mind to me a kingdom is/such present joys therein I find." I believe this was part of the secret of her own great spirit. . . . She was such a joy to live with!"

This is part of the story I wanted to tell the girl who couldn't see how a broad education would help her to "raise" her family.

The Broken Doorsteps

There's an old story about a farm house where the front doorsteps, after years of service, rotted away and had to be removed entirely. The owner intended to replace them but he was busy at the time and he reasoned that the new steps could wait—no one used the front door anyway.

His wife felt less easy about it. It embarrassed her to have their house looking so queer and ill-cared for, with its front door opening in mid-air and a sheer drop of four feet from the sill to the ground. As women do, whenever the time seemed opportune she reminded her husband of the need of new steps; and once, after he had retorted sharply about her "nagging," he made a gesture of repentance by bringing home lumber to build the steps, and piling it beside the house to wait while he went on with more pressing work. Harvest followed seedtime; then it was winter and no season for outdoor carpentry.

In the spring the woman planted flowers about the house as usual, and climbing roses under the parlour windows. "Our place will be prettier than ever—once we get the doorsteps," she told her husband. Later she made a desperate appeal. In June it would be her turn to entertain her church women's group and she just couldn't face it if there were still no steps at the front door. Her husband assured her the steps would be there in time for the party. And then, just before the date, he had a rare opportunity to go with some friends on a fishing trip. It would be his first holiday in ten years, he reminded his wife and dear knows when he would have another. She never mentioned the doorsteps again.

In midsummer, with no warning at all, the woman had a heart attack and died. As the custom was at that time, the funeral service would be held in the home. The undertaker, looking the situation over, turned from the front door to examine the narrow hall leading from the parlour to the back of the house; then he said to the man, "We'll have to have steps at the front. There's no other way to carry the coffin out." Fortunately, the lumber was already at hand. A neighbour came to help and the steps were in place before nightfall.

It's a grim story but a good example of our common lack of response to the needs of those around us, until it is too late to do anything about them.

A toddler follows his mother about the house begging to be picked up, and she thinks, "I mustn't start this or there'll be no end to it." She doesn't know about a small child's actual need of arms around him occasionally. If she would take him up for even a minute he might be happy to go back to playing with the kettle lids again. If she never has time for him he stops asking. Anyway he soon outgrows this particular need of his mother. If he has missed it in his first few years he has missed it for always.

Children come home from school, eager to tell about their day, asking questions not easy to answer. When no one has the interest or the patience to listen, after a while they stop talking; and a few years later a worried father or mother may say: "I haven't the least idea what the boy is thinking; he keeps things to himself"; or, "If she would only confide in me I could help her; but we don't seem to have any common meeting ground any more."

The lonely people, the discouraged and depressed are always with us if we have the discernment to see them. They ask so little—companionship, being made to feel wanted, as necessary to us as we are to them. More than sympathy the discouraged ones may need a build-up of their ego. We think of a school teacher who, after a students' contest, before he congratulated the winner, sought out the others and praised each of them for something good in his effort. Before a sense of failure had time to set in, he was there with an antidote. Somehow this man stands for a host of men and women whose responses are warm and quick to answer a cry for help, even a cry that no one else may hear.

Magic in a Pension Cheque

Millie Ellis sat in her kitchen rocking-chair smiling with incredulous wonder at the piece of cardboard in her hand. She had been expecting it for days; and today when the mailman stopped and left something in the box she had hurried out and there it was—her first Old Age Pension cheque.

Jim Ellis had seen the mailman stop, too, and he came in from the barn, apparently as excited as his wife.

"So it came!" he said. "I was hoping this would be the day. I'm a little short of what it'll take to have the car overhauled. You just have to sign on the back and I can cash it at the bank," he explained.

Millie seemed not to have heard him. "I can't believe it," she said. "Seventy-five dollars of my own!"

"And there'll be another next month," Jim reminded her; "so you don't need to put this away as a curiosity." He examined the cheque judicially. "It's just like mine," he said. "You sign your name here on the back, 'Millicent J. Ellis,' just like it is on the face of the cheque."

Millie took the cheque back but she didn't make any move to endorse it, just sat there starry-eyed as a child before a Christmas tree. Nothing like this had ever happened to her before. Oh, she had inherited five thousand dollars from her grandfather soon after she was married, but she had "never even got to hold it in her hands." It had been put in the bank for her, and Jim persuaded her to let him apply it on the mortgage—he explained how foolish it was to be paying out seven per cent interest when the bank gave only a little over three.

Millie had always wanted a little money of her own, and as a young farm wife she had enlarged her butter and egg trade to the point where sometimes she had a few dollars in cash after the groceries and the children's clothes had been paid for; but very often Jim needed these dollars for machinery repairs or something of the sort. Later the cows and the poultry went into the general farm business, and she had to ask for money as she needed it to run the house. Her sister had received a legacy from their grandfather, too; and she, too, had invested it in the farm—her husband's farm and hers; but it never seemed that she had parted with it. There was no written agreement between them of course but their farming was a partnership with shared responsibilities and a joint bank account.

Strangely enough, as the years passed, Millie, who had practically no experience herself, acquired some shrewd ideas about handling a family income. When her son was about to be married she told him: "If you want to keep your wife as much in love with you after you're married as she is now, sit down with her and plan what you're going to do about money—not just what goes into running the farm, but what will be allotted to run the house, how much for her personal use and for yours." When her daughter decided to keep her job after she was married, Millie advised: "Then don't use your earnings for general expenses. Keep them for the extra piece of furniture you both want, for some improvement about the place, or for savings against an emergency. Don't cheat your husband out of the pride a man takes in supporting his family. Then if the time comes when you have to quit work, it won't be such a shock to him to have to carry the load alone; he'll have been doing it all along."

Millie came out of her daydream apologetically. Jim was still talking and she hadn't been listening.

"Were you saying something, Jim?" she asked.

"I was saying," he replied testily, "that if you'll sign that cheque, I'll take it with me."

Millie smiled good humouredly.

"I wouldn't part with this cheque for anything," she said. "I'm going to cash it myself and spend it myself. Maybe open an account—I've never had a bank account; maybe have a little fling—buy a new dress or get my teeth fixed, or give the grandsons the microscope they've been wanting."

Her husband was fast losing patience. He said, "What's got into you? You never talked like this before."

"It's having a little money of my own," she explained. "You've no idea how independent it makes one feel. And now I can tell you something," she added gently: "I wouldn't have mentioned it before. But sometimes when I needed money and had to ask for it, or when my legacy was gone and we couldn't give the girls music lessons, I would be so bitter I could almost hate you. I hope you didn't notice. But it won't happen again. I'll have my own bit of money and there'll be no blame to you for what's done with it." She was beaming at the cheque again, unworried by any fear of what he might say next. "It's pure magic," she said.

White Christmas

In a Northern settlement where there is always snow on the ground all winter, people sing "I'm dreaming of a white Christmas" with the nostalgia the song seems to stir everywhere. Perhaps they are moved by the Christmas card beauty of the white countryside, but more likely—as with the rest of us—by the thought of a Christmas "just like the ones we used to know." And these memories are not of snow and frost and sleigh-bells, but of warmth and companionship, of loving and being loved.

In our Northern town a few nights before Christmas a very young hockey player trudged home trying hard to keep from crying. All through the game another boy had been giving him sly pokes until he had turned and whacked him over the head. His own father who was the coach had been very sharp about it and had sent him to the bench for the rest of the evening. It meant nothing now that his father was giving him new skates for Christmas if he thought he was a crooked player; likely he was ashamed of him too.

Then the father, walking ahead with some friends, stopped and waited and said, "I know he had it coming to him, son, but you have to learn to hold your temper. I know. I've been through it." So his father understood! He had "been through it" himself. Suddenly everything was right again. Sometimes, years later, under the starlight of a white Christmas, it would all come back to him with a rush of gratitude for the best friend a boy ever had, a father who had given him understanding when he needed it.

The Macdougall farmhouse was lighted at every window. The family were all at home for Christmas. There was no sacrifice they would not make to be together for the holiday. They had gifts of course but these were incidental—the family feeling meant a continuous giving of appreciation and affection and material help if it was needed. The mother, happiest of all, thought "Whatever comes to them later they'll have this to remember."

The Macdougall boys, still keeping ties with their home church, were on their way to the carol service when they saw the son of their German immigrant neighbour come out of a tavern and walk up the street ahead of them. He was turning in at the next tavern when they caught up to him. They had been good friends of the German boy when they were at home, and since they went away he had had no friends except the men he worked with in the mines. He was lonely for young people of his own sort, but his broken English made a barrier. It was good to find the Macdougalls so glad to see him; and when they asked him to come to the carol singing he would have gone with them anywhere.

And how he sang! Most of the carol tunes he knew, and if he sang the words in a different tongue, no one noticed. The Macdougall sitting next to him was so impressed that he suggested they ask Wilhelm to sing "Holy Night" in German. So it was that the people found they had a silver-toned tenor among them—they must have him in the choir. For the first time in his new country the immigrant boy felt wanted; and the turning point would always be associated with "Holy Night" in a little church among friends. He might forget about the white Christmas.

Christmas Is a Family Day.

With the Mercers, Christmas had always been a family day. When they were children they had no grandmothers to visit; and because there were eight of them they pretty well filled a house by themselves, so they stayed at home; and nothing could have suited them better.

They made something special of their celebrations—a decorated tree and carols, a dinner with a turkey as big as the one Scrooge sent to the Cratchits, candles on the table and a sprig of holly in the Christmas pudding. On Christmas eve someone always read the Nativity story from the family Bible, the smaller children crowding close to see the pictures. In the afternoon there would be skating on the pond, the older children helping the little ones, even bundling a toddler into a sleigh and taking him along for a ride. There were gifts, even when times were hard—gifts planned to make those who received them feel happy and loved. If some homeless soul could be found to share the day with them, the hospitality was a family affair—just another part of their good day together.

As the family grew up they left home, but they always came back for Christmas; and these homecomings were the highlight of the holiday for everyone. When someone went to meet the train on Christmas eve the littlest one would watch from the window till it was too dark to see; then she would listen for the car rattling over the bridge down the road and would rush out to meet it coming up the lane.

Later the same child was to know the catch in the throat of the homecomer at the picture every son and daughter knew so well—their mother standing against the lamplight at the kitchen door, waiting—a picture they would remember as long as they lived.

These people had never heard about members of a family being unable to "communicate." Sometimes a friend might say, "I can't talk to my mother" or "My brother won't listen to me." This was hard for them to understand. When they came home for Christmas they couldn't talk fast enough and everyone listened—all concerned if one had a problem, interested in everyone's plans and hopes, inordinately proud of one another and not afraid to show it. And their mother who had nurtured this feeling from childhood knew that when she was no longer with them no one would feel alone. If trouble came to one of them, they would all stand up to it together like a square of Gordon Highlanders.

There was the first terrible Christmas after Ben was killed in the war—Ben who was such a tower of strength, trying to take a father's place in the family, who was so gay and good-looking and promising, the pride of them all. Back in the old home the reminders of him at every turn were almost unbearable. As usual it was their mother who comforted them. She who had always been so orthodox about such things said now:

"Anyone as close to us as Ben was isn't far away now, I think. Remember the year he was working with the surveyors and he walked all night to get home for Christmas. Caring about us as he did and knowing how we loved him he just couldn't stay away. . . . And what a good time we had that year!"

It was a great help to have such times to remember. It was good, too, to have these memories years later when the brothers and sisters spent Christmas in their own homes with their own children; when the mother was gone and there was no home centre to go to anymore. And to the one who did not have a family of her own, the child who had watched at the window on Christmas eve, the recollection gave a meaning to life that she might have missed altogether without it.

THE CHANGING COUNTRYSIDE

A Feeling for the Farm

They have moved the old Peter McArthur house from the farm at Appin, Ontario, to the Pioneer Village of Doon, where it can be preserved and cared for in memory of a writer whose every word was awaited eagerly by the farm people of this country a few decades ago.

At that time Peter McArthur, essayist, poet, critic, editor, had made a place for himself among writers in New York and Britain. It was a hunger for a simpler, happier life that brought him with his young family back to the farm his father had cleared from the woods of Middlesex county. And it was then Peter McArthur began to write about country things. Perhaps his experience in more sophisticated places gave him the perspective to see what those who have always lived in the country might overlook. Anyway, he opened up for farm people a world of interest and entertainment, a scope for humour and philosophy right at their doors. Commenting on the antics of a cat inside his kitchen window and a kitten outside, the cat switching his tail and the kitten trying to catch it through the glass, he wrote: "Why is it that a little by-play like this between a cat and a kitten can cause more hearty and wholesome laughter in a normal family than they could get at a comedy or a picture show?"

He wrote of human nature in turkeys, of how his flock took

153

to roosting on the ridge pole of the cow stable, and the gobbler who insisted on roosting at the extreme north end always flew up at the south end, pushing his way along the roof, pecking the others out of his way and finally settling down "with all the dignity of a dowager who has disturbed a seatful of music lovers at a concert."

Through Peter McArthur's columns, readers came to feel well acquainted with his farm animals—the Red Cow who, if she could not get over a fence or through it could always get under, the inquisitive ram, Socrates, Bildad, the pup; and many a family began to find interesting characters in their own flocks and herds. There was his observation of the lambs playing King of the Castle, "bunting one another from the roof of an empty hen coop"; and his apology for the momentary commercial thought that such fun should be filmed for the movies.

And how this farmer poet could kindle an awareness of things most of us overlook in the natural world around us! There was his advice on how to get a change of air and a change of scene by getting up at a different hour in the morning, the story of the domestic row in a family of screech-owls, the report of all hands stopping work to listen to a mockingbird singing from a thorn tree in the next field.

"Besides providing a livelihood, farming offers possibilities of spiritual and mental culture beyond any other occupation"— this McArthur philosophy is reflected in his feeling for his own land. Working in the sugar bush, he wrote: "I was conscious of the companionship of my trees for I have known them since I was a boy." And again: "I remembered coasting with a home-made sled on a little bank beside the creek and also remembered seeing my children coasting on that same bank on sleds of their own making."

It is regrettable that Peter McArthur's books are out of print, that they could not be saved, like his house. Happily, here and there we still find something of his feeling for the farm.

The Memorial Window

The artist, an old man now and living far from the home of his youth in the Valley, wanted to give a stained-glass window to the church. He wrote that he owed a great debt to the people of the Valley for what they had taught him about one of the hardest things a man has to learn—how to be a neighbour to his fellowman. He remembered how the farmers had shared their work and the women had helped each other through sickness and trouble; their kindness to the unfortunate, such as the boy who would always be a child—the boy liked to go visiting and there wasn't a home in the Valley where he was not made welcome.

The artist was sure this spirit still lived in the Valley and he wanted to picture it in a church window. He even sent a sketch of his design and it was lovely—the background unmistakably the sweep of the Valley with its fields and farmsteads, the beautiful old stone church, and in the foreground, on a road leading up the hill, a traveller reaching out to help another with his burden.

The people were touched that one of their sons should feel so warmly about the life he remembered. "But that was a long time ago," they said. "There isn't much neighbouring now, nor the same need for it." They were not sure they could be classed with the traveller easing the load of his neighbour. Farming today was a business and a man had to fend for himself.

"Neighbours used to do a man's work if he was sick," someone remembered. "We still do," a Valley farmer said. And a visitor from outside reminded them that when the new Russian immigrant was taken ill in seeding time, he was surprised one morning to see a dozen men with tractors in his fields putting in his crop. "A Russian from a country under suspicion by most people in the West!" the visitor said. "Even the good-hearted pioneers might not have been so ready to help him."

There were still people in the Valley who could remember women nursing their neighbours through sickness, doing their best with the amateur skill they had. Then they found a better way. They had a co-operative hospital plan long before the government took it up, and later a sort of pooled medicare. "But the help isn't personal, like it used to be," someone argued, recalling a story from the deadly cholera days, of a woman who, fully aware of the danger, went into a stricken home and took care of the family, single handed. "You don't find people risking their lives for their neighbours nowadays." "Sure you do," another protested. "Remember how young Allen, when his hired man's house was burning, bolted in and got the children out seconds before the roof fell in."

But the friendliness! Would doors be opened to a retarded boy in these days? Everyone agreed that no doubt they would, if he could catch anyone at home. Just now the women were taking turns driving another child to a special school.

Just as it was decided to accept the window, they remembered that they would have no place to put it. To ensure a continuing church they had voted to go into a larger parish and at the end of the year the old church they loved would be closed or sold or wrecked. Or would it? Couldn't they keep it for an occasional meeting-place, a place with a rare memorial window, a reminder of a great tradition, a guide for the years ahead?

Smoke from My Neighbour's Chimney

On a corner of the farm there was a little house where an old woman lived. She had asked to move in because she had no other place to go and no money to pay rent. And the child in the farm house noticed that every morning her mother looked to see if there was smoke coming from the chimney of the little house. A smoking chimney meant that the old woman was stirring and able to start her fire. If there was no smoke the little girl would be sent on some errand; perhaps to take the old woman a few eggs or a pail of fresh buttermilk, and her mother would say, "Knock on the door and if there is no answer don't go in but come right back and tell me."

Soon the girl was old enough to understand that her mother was watching over their neighbour without letting her know. She would not hurt the old woman's pride by making her feel she was a care to anyone, nor frighten her with the thought that at her age she might take a stroke in the night or fall and break a hip. But if such misfortune should befall, her neighbour would be on hand to take care of her.

Chimney watching was a common custom in the country some years ago and we still hear of it occasionally, though a telephone call may be more practical now. Indeed in apartment houses for old people, the residents who live alone very often take turns in making a morning telephone survey to see that no one has been taken ill in the night. But there is still a place for the secret surveillance of watching for a neighbour's chimney smoke without letting our concern worry him.

There is the school nurse who discovers a nervous trouble that a child manages to hide from everyone else, who says nothing to disturb the child but goes direct to those who can do something about it—his parents or his teachers. Some teachers, too, have a gift for discovering the hidden hurts in a youngster and enlisting the help of his family. And of course an endless number of fathers and mothers are grappling with influences in the school and the community that are upsetting their children. Some of them may not be as wise as they would like to be in handling these problems. Others seem to be naturals at anything that has to do with rearing children. All working together could be as effective as a township brigade of chimney watchers.

The year Ben Houghton's barn was burned and his son had to have a lot of costly surgery to save a leg crushed by a tractor, everyone knew that Ben was in desperate need of money. He had never borrowed a dollar in his life; anyway he wouldn't know where to turn for a loan and none of his neighbours could help him. But one of them had an idea. In the parishes around, the people had credit unions where they deposited their savings and borrowed when they needed funds. Now was the time to start a local union and get Ben to join, presumably because they needed members with a reputation for stability. Once he was a member Ben would learn that it was a service to the credit union to borrow from it—that the only dividends the members received came from interest (at reasonable rates) on loans. Perhaps Ben would never know that the credit union was set up at this particular time to help him without making him feel dependent.

The field of the chimney watcher seems boundless. Someone notices that the neighbourhood boys who dropped out of school are at loose ends, picking up odd jobs as they can find them, getting nowhere. Instead of blaming the school system, the neighbour gets a trade school to set up night classes in the community, hoping some of the boys may be drawn into skilled occupations. Leaders of organizations see that some individual or family or several families of newcomers from another country are being left out of the community life and they find irresistibly appealing ways of bringing them in. A woman with a mother's heart and clever hands feels a concern for the motherless little girl, lonely, tired, often discouraged, trying to keep up at school and keep house for her family; for the girl whose home is not what it should be and who would like to make it better; for the new Canadian girls whose education stopped with public school but who want to learn more and have a place in their new country. The woman can't go into their homes and say, "Try this way"; so she brings them together with others in a 4-H Homemaking Club, shows them how to cook and sew and make friends and grow in grace and character. . . . For chimney watchers don't just stand and look at a smokeless chimney. They usually act with the speed and efficiency—but not the noise—of a fire brigade.

A Folkway Worth Saving

Again they have held their annual Old Time Fiddlers' Contest at Shelburne, Ontario, with an audience drawn from far beyond the county and fiddlers from almost every province in the Dominion, even from across the border, down Kentucky way.

Every year some of the virtuosos at the final concert come from the South and these seem to make a point of showing us just what a fiddle can do—having us holding our breath at the beauty of Mendelssohn's "Spring Song," foot-tapping to "Turkey in the Straw," or listening incredulously to the wind in the trees or the frogs in the marshes. Our own fiddlers have their repertoire too. Often there is a class for serious music, and usually an opening for a bit of humour—the drone of the bagpipes, plucked strings in "Pop Goes the Weasel." And what some of our fiddlers can do with "Listen to the Mockingbird!" This year they had the birds twittering as I had never heard them before—a brilliant performance.

But most of the program is given to music for the old traditional dances—jigs and reels and waltzes and others, since playing for these dances has been the chief function of the fiddler in this country from pioneer times to the present, or at least until dance halls became too large for the squeak of the fiddle to be heard above the stamp or shuffle of the dancers' feet, or until people felt rich enough to hire an orchestra. Stephen Vincent Benet's memory of the neighbours dancing in the backwoods cabin of his childhood might be the experience of many a country child over this continent. He says:

> I can hear them dance like a foggy song
> Through the deepest one of my slumbers,
> The fiddle squeaking the boots along
> And my father calling the numbers.
> The quick feet shaking the puncheon floor,
> The fiddle squeaking and squealing,
> Till the dried herbs rattled above the door
> And the dust went up to the ceiling.

In the early days of the West when the prairie "shack" had little space for a dance floor, homesteaders came from all directions to dances in the school house—these were about the only social events they had; and no one thought of a dance without a fiddler, or better, two, so they could "spell each other off" as the dance went on from dark to daybreak. All winter the dance and the fiddle made the neighbourhood frolic in the habitants' homes of French Canada. To the annual Festival of the Arts in Nova Scotia, little groups from all over the province bring their dances as well as their crafts and their music. Some of the small towns have resident dancing teachers and their dancing —square dancing, folk dancing, national and ballroom dancing— is an art as well as a pleasure.

And is it possible that the old fiddle tunes have done something to preserve the traditional dances that have been with us always? For even while gyrations borrowed from the savages have come and gone, the courtly old-time quadrilles and reels and waltzes have lasted—and always they have been associated with the fiddler.

The square dance and fiddling are among our oldest folkways. Perhaps their own appeal will ensure their survival for another century. Still, it seems good to have such occasional revivals as the Nova Scotia Festival and the Old Time Fiddlers' Contest.

Neighbours

The Wilkses had a flair for neighbouring. In the years when there was a home on every hundred acres in the settlement, their parlour was the one most often lighted in the evening— people liked to visit them. If sickness came to a neighbour, Jane Wilks was at the door in no time to see if her help was needed.

The Wilkses were close to their neighbours in the little

church where they met every Sunday, worshipped together, held their socials and felt that it was good to be among friends. And they had a sort of family pride in one another. A visitor from "outside" was likely to hear about the especially successful farmer, the young people who went away and distinguished themselves in the world, the families who were good community people like the Wilkses who had done so much for the school, had started the library and who were such good neighbours.

Jane Wilkse's granddaughter, Janie, was one of the girls who left the neighbourhood for a career of her own, did a stint at social work in the city and came back to marry her high school sweetheart, Jim Elder. Jim's farm now included the old Wilks place and half a dozen others—here as everywhere else the small farms had disappeared and with them had gone the families that made a populous closely-knit neighbourhood.

Jane Wilks, coming to visit her granddaughter, could have wept at the change. "Why, you have no neighbours!" she said. "Even the church and the school have gone; and it used to be such a fine neighbourhood." But soon she came to see that Janie had neighbours in unexpected places.

Janie didn't visit much with her friends—many of the younger women had both jobs and families and little time for visiting. But they met in clubs and committees, most of which had to do with the school or the church or the community centre—all concerns of the neighbourhood. They seemed to be especially friendly with the foreign-born women finding their way in a new land. (Jane could remember how upset she had been when refugees from Europe bought farms bordering on the old settlement.) And there seemed to be no town and country distinction any more. Janie had a lot in common with the town librarian and the school psychologist; and now that farming had become big business, Jim found the bank manager as much his neighbour as the men who used to come to help on threshing day.

Jane had always tried to "make allowance" for neighbours' boys who got drunk and made trouble occasionally; Janie, working through the Centre, was trying to give boys such interests that they wouldn't want to get drunk. Jane had not hesitated to help nurse a family through diphtheria; Jane and her friends organized clinics to immunize children so they wouldn't have diphtheria. Jane had never been too busy to be nice to her neighbour's little retarded girl; Janie and others were seeing that retarded children had the sort of school they needed.

It was rather a shock to Jane to see her granddaughter visiting regularly at the mental hospital. She remembered, when one of her old neighbours "had to be put away," how the people spoke of it in whispers. Now the women's clubs were trying to help mental patients back to health, mixing with them at social affairs. Jane and others of her time had been good to destitute old people—taking them a meal occasionally, seeing that they had firewood. Since then people had not only pressed the government into providing Homes; every organization seemed to be doing something to make these Homes more homelike for the old folks. Janie was a personal friend of some of the loneliest. She still had neighbours.

Country Lanes

To anyone who likes walking, either as a way of getting from one place to another or for the sheer enjoyment of it, country roads today offer little comfort. Where can you walk? Either in the ditch or so close to the traffic that each passing car is a hazard. No wonder we remember the days when every road had its worn foot path along the side, when its course veered to avoid such obstacles as a rocky hill or a pond or a stand of heavy timber, and we could wonder what might be around the bend.

Our country roads were "rolling," like the land—not pared down to the monotonous level of a highway. They might wind up a mountain in such leisurely steps that you scarcely knew you were climbing, or face you with a sharp little rise to take your breath away. There were variations in light and shadow, too. Here and there stretches of forest gave shelter from the heat of summer or the winds of winter; or a road might narrow to pass between walls of damp, mossy rock, then broaden again in the sunlight of open country.

Sometimes a tiny stream trickled down from a spring in the hills; and always there were roadside flowers. In the spring a few violets strayed out from the woods and, as the seasons passed, there were may-apples and daisies and columbines and Queen Anne's lace and goldenrod and purple asters and dock and milkweed. Chokecherry and wild plum and apple trees blossomed in the spring and children stopped for their fruit in summer.

There were other diversions, such as a bridge over a creek where you could lean on the railing and watch the minnows in the water. Sometimes we met a "horse and rig" and occasionally a car. Usually we recognized the horse before we could see the people but they were mostly folk we knew and they might stop for a few words.

I remember, too, a prairie trail in Saskatchewan where there were no woods or creeks or rocky passes, but where prairie chickens came out of the grass to run ahead of the horses in the wheel tracks and where crocuses and briar roses grew wild in the spring. I suppose like the country roads in Ontario, these prairie trails have gone too.

From roads we turned into country lanes. Most of the lanes I know haven't changed much. There is still the gravelled drive with its neat grass borders, and along the fences trees planted by a grandfather years and years ago. Sometimes the fence is a stone wall, another monument to the labour of the pioneers.

Most old lanes were long because settlers liked their buildings to have a central location on the farm. On one farm in our township the house could not be seen from the road at all; but it was a large house and a popular place for the "beef ring" to hold its annual oyster supper. Going to one of these gatherings on a dark November night, we turned in at the road gate and drove for what seemed a mile before we came to a beautiful, big, stone house lighted from cellar to garret, a warm, hospitable, comfortable home. I wonder what became of that lane when farmers began to drive cars in winter. Cars and the Canadian snowfall have pretty well out-dated the lovely, long farm lane.

So, for one reason or another, we have few good country paths for walking any more, few places to enjoy the sights and sounds of the natural world around us. Some people try to make up for this by having walks through a woodlot, some by getting into the crusade for conservation. Some farmers take their holidays among the northern lakes and forests, or go hunting in the fall. Children especially compensate a little through nature books and movies. Many families try to create a sort of "green belt" around their homes, with trees and flowers and something of a bird sanctuary, as well as a sanctuary for themselves. Then after a hard drive on the highway, it's "Oh for the gate and the locust lane and dusk and dew and home again!" There's still the lane.

"The Crick"

We called it "the crick," a clean, free-running stream, turbulent as a river in springtime and never going dry in the hottest summer. It had its beginning where water from a millpond fell over a dam with the roar of a little Niagara, found itself in a rocky, level channel and slackened its pace to meander through the fields. As it travelled it wound its course around rocks and hillocks, loitered in bays where the bank was soft, hurried where the channel hardened and deepened, slipping over stones in silvery waterbreaks.

The creek travelled through pasture fields where cows came down to drink; through woods where wild ducks had their nests and out into the open where we sometimes saw a blue heron midstream or a crane standing on one leg camouflaged like a bundle of sticks. The stream deepened into pools where children learned to swim—and always it kept moving, its ripples flashing in the sun.

There was one spot that I knew well. Here the gravelly bottom was firm though rough to bare feet. The sun made dappled patterns on the sand, minnows came and nibbled at our toes, and to wade in the cold, shallow water was a thrilling adventure for a small child. The road passed right through the creek at this point—there was another way with a bridge, but farmers sometimes liked to drive through the water to tighten the metal tires on the wood of their wagon wheels or to give their horses a drink.

Flowers grew along "the crick"—snapdragons and tigerlilies and in the spring patches of marsh-marigolds. Where the stream was clear and cold as spring water we gathered watercress, our earliest "greens" of the season. And peppermint. What child living near a creek doesn't know the delightful combination of peppermint leaves and a drink of cold water? There were speckled trout in the creek too, beautiful, silvery fish flecked with red, a delicacy that brought fishermen from the towns for miles around.

All of this is only a memory now, for the creek has disappeared as though it had never been, except for the ugly scar where the stream bed used to be, now dry as dust, littered with debris and overgrown in places with weeds and tough little weed trees. One year at the time of the spring freshet someone neglected to take the top plank from the dam, and in the night the whole countryside was wakened by a crash and a roar as the barricade was splintered into matchwood and tons of water poured over the flats below. Fortunately there were no dwellings in the way, but fields were flooded, and bridges miles downstream were washed away. By midsummer the last trickle of the stream had dried in the sun and what was left of the pond was a mosquito-breeding marsh.

The loss of our creek was so dramatic that we will never forget it; but other creeks are disappearing all over the country and most people don't seem to know what is happening. We have all heard, of course, that creeks fail where trees have been cut and the water from rain and snow tears down slopes carrying the soil with it, flooding the land in spring and leaving it washed out and dry in summer. And we know vaguely that streams have a role wherever there are hills and valleys. Yet perhaps we have never asked a conservation authority if there is something we can do to save the goodness and beauty of the land around us. But of course, some people don't know what it means to live beside a creek.

Good-bye to the Little Red School

"Still sits the school house by the road/a ragged beggar sleeping;/around it still the sumachs grow/and blackberry vines are creeping"—one of the derelict old roadside schools, forsaken and left to decay in its own fashion.

A stranger parked his car in the yard, tried the door and walked in—transients had broken the lock years ago. There had been other tenants, too; squirrels had left a litter of acorn shells; a bird had come in at a broken window, couldn't find its way out and lay dead on the floor. But the teacher's desk was in its place with the old globe now obsolete after two world wars. The box stove was rusted but ashes of old fires were still on the hearth; and the battered old seats had not been moved.

The man stood beside the desk that had been his sixty years ago, and the ghosts of other children appeared in their places.

Many were dead now, some he only vaguely remembered, but he had followed the careers of a few and it was strange how many who had shown no special promise at school had grown into successful, even brilliant men and women. He knew well what it might have meant to them if their abilities had been discovered early, but the old school courses did not encourage special gifts. As an educationist in the years since, he had helped to change this and some of the changes had their beginnings in this tumble-down school.

It came back to him now—his discomfort in school at the beginning, his fear of the teacher and the "big boys," his confusion about what was expected of him, because the teacher did little actual teaching. Teachers were such as the trustees could get for the salary they offered and there were good, bad and indifferent. One was a wizard at mathematics and neither knew or cared much about anything else. In the new township schools almost every teacher was a specialist so a youngster might have a good teacher for about everything he had to learn. Among the good things of the old days were the "readers," taken mostly from the classics. When he heard public men of his own generation quote glibly from Gray's "Elegy" or "Horatius" he suspected they knew the lines, not because they were poetry fans but because they had memorized them at school.

Of course the school had had a few "born" teachers. The man would never forget the year his mother was in the hospital. Home was desolate and the future bleak; but he could forget his troubles in school. . . . The teacher had ways of comforting his fears, keeping his mind busy and lifting his spirits—the sort of teacher the man later tried to find for "disturbed" children.

He remembered—of course he had never forgotten—the teacher who had talked to him about a vocation. Teaching was not a well-paid job at that time but this teacher never mentioned salary—just talked about the dearth of good teachers and the satisfaction of helping a child who needed help. Where, the man wondered, could such counsellors be found today.

When it was closed the old school's attendance had dwindled to a listless little half dozen children needing the stimulation of numbers. In its overcrowded days it had been a "rough" school. The man remembered how a retarded boy had been teased, a German family ostracized in wartime. Now in his grandchildren's school the eighth graders had set up a committee for a "just society" to take care of such problems. He supposed the idea came from discussions in their social studies. Country children would learn more about social action in their new schools.

The man still had a few friends from among the boys of his school days; he had long since lost touch with any of the girls. Compared with present boy and girl associations it was amusing and rather nice to think of how shy the boys were with girls as they got into the teen years. He remembered walking the long road home after school, singing in a boy's uncertain voice a song that was new then, "The Trail of the Lonesome Pine." He was alone and singing to himself, but really to a very special girl, though she was nowhere within hearing. It didn't matter now, of course, but he was rather sorry there had been no social doings at school so that he might have known her better.

The desks were carved with initials he might know but he went away without stopping to read them. He could not feel nostalgic for the old school. Some schools deserved this, he knew; but his had been only run-of-the-mill. His job was to work for something better.

Conversation Pieces

We were watching a showing of slides taken on a family holiday, and our host loaned us polaroid glasses. Immediately the pictures came alive in a way that reminded me of something I had not thought of in years— the old stereoscope on the parlour table with its little collection of "views."

I still remember the stir this simple device created in our neighbourhood. A young agent, presumably earning money to go to college, rode a bicycle up and down the country roads, selling a stereoscope and a few pictures at most of the farm houses; and for some evenings thereafter neighbours visited around just to see each other's pictures. A few were coloured— these were more expensive, but lovely. I remember a green country lane bordered by a stone fence overgrown with pink roses; and in the foreground a pretty girl leading a Jersey calf. There were "comic" subjects, too, innocent enough by today's standards, but at that time usually shown with a word of apology. Altogether the stereoscope was considered quite a discovery in home entertainment. On a Sunday afternoon it was a pleasant pastime to sit in the parlour and re-view the pictures; but after a while we looked at them only when we showed them to visitors. They gave us something to talk about.

Before this of course we had the family album as a conversation piece. The album was primarily an archive for the family portraits, just as the family Bible preserved a record of births, marriages and deaths, but it was a common custom on a social call in the neighbourhood to have someone "show us the photos." Personally I never tired of seeing family pictures. The commentary that went with them often made an intriguing story, enlivened as it was by such visual aids.

Some time after the stereoscope, came the picture postcard fad, and friends who would never have thought of writing a letter if they left home for a few days, seized the opportunity to send a postcard. Almost every girl had an album for these cards; or they could be displayed on a wire wall-rack to be looked over like pictures in an art gallery—a never failing subject for conversation.

With amateur photography came snapshots, pictures that might take on a significance in the years ahead—children from babyhood up, family gatherings, weddings, holidays with friends. It is almost unbelievable, the history to be found in one snapshot album—dress fashions over fifty years or more; transportation from the horse and buggy to late model cars; things that soon will have passed out of memory, such as a field of stooked wheat. Old albums may be stored away and forgotten except for occasional reference, but what talking pieces they were in their day!

Now we have colour photography and slides; and amateur travelogues are one of our popular forms of entertainment. In an informal home setting there is likely to be audience participation all along the way. What next, I wonder. No doubt some device yet unheard of will soon give us something else to talk about. Or is it possible the time will come when our communications will come from ideas or feeling or wonderings within ourselves? I am not thinking of a clever dialogue or a debate or a dissertation by some brilliant conversationist—just good talk where, to quote Samuel Johnson, "there is no competition, no vanity, but a calm, quiet interchange of sentiments"—and this without a visual aid or any other prop.

Vacation Time

At a time when most city people are off on wheels or lakes or playgrounds, farmers are at their busiest. Farm women are busy too; but except where the load of work is more than anyone should have to carry, there are few complaints. And they have learned to live as they go—taking something from the days as well as giving to them.

A few years ago the Associated Country Women of the World had an essay competition on "A Country Woman's Day." For women north of the equator the time of writing was midsummer so the days were well filled with work. And one must have been speaking for many, when, after a staggering review of her day's cooking, washing, ironing, giving a hand with the milking, picking berries and getting them into the freezer, caring for children and chickens, a social half-hour with the family, then putting the small ones to bed, she wrote: "Not all days are like this, for I have a flexible time table. Sometimes my work waits as I think,

> What is this life if full of care
> We have no time to stand and stare?

Several writers stressed the importance of taking time now and then to "stand and stare." Some found this time in their flower gardens. An hour squeezed from housework or farmwork to create a bit of beauty around them was recreation.

Work was lightened, too, by the companionship of working with the family. From the essays it seems that the farmer's wife is ready to do whatever she can to help him. "After all, it's our living," one woman explained. Another wrote: "I end the day with a deep feeling of thankfulness that I have health and enjoyment in sharing the work with my husband." Other comments were: "There were other boys who could have given me more material things but they couldn't compare with Jim for mental hospitality. The wonderful talks we have!" "We must feed and water the chickens. What fun that is for a three-year-old!" And, "After the dishes are done comes the children's hour of music and stories."

A fact made clear in these essays was that most country women like the country. A woman going to the orchard with the children to pick apples looked up and saw a flock of migrating hawks "wheeling and circling by the hundreds," and called the boys to look, "hoping that in the years to come they would keep their minds open to enjoy such sights." Again we read: "When I opened the door hundreds of blackbirds chirped in the trees by the river. How I love this early morning hour!" And this: "I am tired tonight but only healthfully so. How lovely it is with the murmuring night sounds and the tinkle of a neighbour's cow-bell; The moon has risen and is silvering the world with magic." Would anyone on vacation in the northern woods find more beauty in the night than this?

With all her summer work the farm woman does not give up her interests outside herself—her church, her Sunday school class, her neighbours. Giving an idea of the range of these interests, a woman told about going to her mailbox and finding the daily paper, a farm magazine, the church women's study book and the latest review from a readers' club. One started the dinner cooking then "brushed up on" the music she would play at a wedding.

A country woman's summer is no holiday. But it can be a fine spell of living.

History Repeats

The Bishops were a family who believed in education. Bishop men for years back had graduated from universities in the Old Land, and even the women had learned something of the humanities along with the social graces. So when Benjamin Bishop, two hundred years ago came to Canada in the British civil service, it was natural that he should bring a tutor for his children. He was taking no chance on the educational facilities he might find in the new country.

Everyone knew, of course, that there were many Canadian children out of reach of a school of any sort. Where there *were* schools, interested parents paid a tuition fee. Some families had no money to pay a fee; and some saw no reason for sending a boy to school when he was needed at home to help clear the land. Sometimes Mr. Bishop in his public speeches made a plea for night classes for men who had had no schooling in their youth.

Then, of all things, some "fanatic" started a crusade for public schools providing free education for *all* children—and not only *free* but *compulsory*, with everyone sharing the cost through taxes! To some families this seemed "an answer to prayer." To others it was a threat to their right to bring up their children without interference from the government. And the Bishops, in spite of their appreciation of education for themselves, were as outraged as anyone and more vocal than most.

"In the first place the country couldn't afford it," they argued. (The reply came back that the country couldn't afford to stumble along with a population half illiterate.) "With schools springing up everywhere there wouldn't be enough teachers to go round." "People would impose on the privilege—great, hulking lads who couldn't read or write coming to school. No teacher could do her best work with such a mob."

The Bishops, being people of influence, were able to keep free public education out of their area for some time—until their neighbours saw how well it worked in more progressive places.

Some generations later a number of the Bishops' descendants were medical doctors. They were good doctors, too, always with a large practice and corresponding income; but no one knew how much service they gave that they were never paid for. No one knew, either, how many people with limited means put off seeing them because they couldn't pay their bills; how many illnesses progressed beyond help through this delay; how many children grew up with defects that could have been corrected. And if a family were hit by catastrophic medical expenses that took their savings, their home, their farm or their business, little was said about it. When one of the family is ill he must have the help he needs regardless of cost.

The time came when some "radicals" pointed out that under a health insurance plan a family could pay the same amount spread over years in taxes without losing everything they had. Then all the century-old arguments against state education were brought out against state health service. "The country couldn't afford it." "There wouldn't be enough doctors to go round." "People would take advantage of it." "Doctors couldn't do their best work." "It meant state dictation in personal affairs." Not a word about the state seeing a child's right to health as well as education.

So, as with state education, state health service is delayed here and there; but it will arrive. "Nothing can stop an idea whose hour has come."

The Old Orchard

The man looked up from the letter he was reading and the view from his office window changed from a skyline of apartments and office buildings to a blur of apple trees—apple trees in blossom; apple trees in October heavy with fruit, bare black apple trees etched against the snow of winter. He saw again the stone farmhouse at the end of the lane with the orchard in the foreground as it was on most farms in the country of his youth; and he thought no landscape architect had ever designed anything more pleasant or fitting. Now his brother had written:

"We've cut down the old orchard. Unless you're growing apples commercially you can't afford either the time or the money to take care of an orchard."

The man was back again in his childhood, on a spring evening standing in wonder before the crab-apple tree, incredibly lovely in its shimmering white among the other trees, like a bride with her pink tinted attendants. This was the season when bees hummed in the blossoms like an orchestra tuning and birds were everywhere, some of them nesting in the same tree year after year. He could not remember when he learned the way to the trees very special to a child—the first early harvest apples and the "sweet bough" tree; the favourite St. Lawrence, comforting to take along when he had to go back to school at the end of summer; the snow apples always ripe for Hallowe'en. There were the "winter apples" that had to be picked while they were still too hard to eat but red as berries and scenting the air like wine. Every fall a barrel of these was sent to the brother on a homestead in the West. They were more than apples to him; they were a bit of home.

The orchard had provided fruit for the table the year round. The first apple pie of the summer was cause for a family celebration. Apple pie was a staple in the Saturday baking from fall to spring. A bowl of applesauce came to the table as regularly as the teapot—except for company meals when it gave way to something less plebeian. And on winter evenings when the family gathered around the fire to read, someone always brought a dish of apples from the cellar. For years after he left the farm the man had the idea that the crunching of an apple went with the reading of a book.

Toward spring the apples in the cellar had wilted a little and the family felt they had lost the best of their flavour; then they wanted the sharp, fresh tang of *dried* apples. Their mother knew this would come; so every year when the tart fall apples were ready, she would get all hands busy in the evenings at a "paring bee." The sliced apples were carefully dried over the kitchen stove and put away until spring. And the city man's palate, jaded with the fare of gourmet restaurants, quickened at the recollection of a warm, spicy, home-dried apple pie.

The orchard mirage still hung over the city, changing with the changing seasons. Now it was spring again and another child would be gazing starry-eyed at the white crab-apple tree. But the tree wouldn't be there! What was happening to the country? Once it was a happy place for children, a place where there were woods and streams and fields—and orchards. His brother's family would live on a farm as regimented as a factory. They couldn't even have an apple orchard because everything had to pay its way and an orchard took too many man-hours for spraying. He went back to his letter and read:

"The place looks bare with the apple-trees gone but already Bob has started replanting with something he's had in mind for a while back. In a few years he'll take over the farm. He'll be married and his children will grow up here. Maybe already he's thinking about this, wanting them to see more of the natural world than even most country children do now. So where the old orchard was, he's starting a bird sanctuary—has most of the trees planted but they'll take a while to grow. Sometimes I think the young people today have more imagination than we had."

The Old Church Closes

The old church stood at the crossroads in a shelter of pines, its well-kept graveyard stretching into the field at the back. Twice the cemetery had been extended to meet the community's need. The stone walls were as firm as when a local mason built them more than a century ago, the high-pitched roof and the arched windows as classic and timeless as their prototypes in the Old Land where churches were built to last for generations. Now the old church was to be closed because the congregation was too small either to support it or to justify keeping it open.

On an October evening Martha Wall, an old and loyal member, parked her car at the roadside as one who might have come to say good-bye to an old friend. Sunset blazoned the windows with gold. The pines cast long black shadows on the grass. Martha could remember, as a girl, coming out from an evening service and standing, breathless, at the beauty of the same shadows in the moonlight.

There had been no evening service for years now; and it seemed only yesterday that it had been a trysting-place for young lovers from all over the district. Even in the mornings there were now only a handful of worshippers where once the pews had been crowded with families from grandparents to babies. After the service they would loiter to "visit" for a while or to talk over the sermon. They had good preachers in those days, Martha recalled—mature, scholarly men of faith and conviction. Usually they stayed long enough to get to know their people, to take a personal interest in the children. Men and women were still grateful for some minister's counsel when they needed it. More than one bright youngster had been given an education because the minister advised it.

Today, all the farm children went to high school and most of them into callings other than farming. Mechanization demanded larger farms so small farmers sold their land and moved away. Where there had once been thirty families there were now not more than ten. The school had already been closed and the children transferred to a central school. Now the church would go and the congregation would be expected to join the church in town.

Martha wondered if the experts who talked so glibly about "the waste of manpower on the rural circuit," the growth of "the ecumenical spirit" and the "pooling of resources," knew what it meant to give up the church that had been hers all her life. She had been born into it; had had a place in the Sunday School and the choir, had learned the catechism and in due course had become a member. The social life of her youth had centred in the church; her children had been christened and married there.

And it had been such an "active" church with its thriving organizations, its concerts and suppers that had drawn crowds from miles away. The concerts had gone out of fashion years ago and the gourmet suppers could never be managed by the few women who were left. In the crossroads church there had passed a glory from the earth.

Oh, it hadn't been fair weather all the way. Martha could dimly remember a furore over something called "higher criticism," almost as divisive as the new curriculum. Disputes had been bitter and personal and one family had left the church; but Martha had been young then and divisions didn't affect the young people much—they were having too good a time being together. Remembering this, it occurred to Martha that, like herself, her children had had the social life of their youth in the church; this was where their marriages were made. Where would her grandsons turn for friends? And then she remembered that there were few girls in the congregation any more and her grandsons' friends were the young people they had met in high school and later in youth interests over a wider area. They would find them again in the central church.

Martha thought of a presbytery meeting she had just attended in town. After the last year of whatever supply could be found for the crossroads pulpit, it had been good to hear the able, stirring addresses. She had liked the women, too, and the things they were doing, such as the after-school centre for children of working mothers. Perhaps she could help with that —she was an old hand at making "pieces" for children after school.

A cool little wind stirred in the pine trees; the sun went down and dusk began to settle over the old church. Its era had almost ended—but not quite, Martha thought. It had laid a foundation to build on. It would have to be closed but it should not be left a prey to neglect. Perhaps at least as long as the old members lived, it could be kept as an occasional meeting place, the centre of a historic burial-ground, a memorial to a source of the people's pride in their past.

The Quilt and Rug Fair

The Simcoe County Quilt and Rug Fair draws visitors from miles away; and the quilts and rugs make a brave and colourful showing. Viewed closely, most of the exhibits are models of workmanship and a sophisticated use of design and colour. The old patterns, Irish Chain, Dresden Plate, Double Wedding Ring and the others, are reproduced with a respect for tradition; and the original designs show imagination and sometimes considerable art. A new "centennial quilt" gives an authentic reproduction of "Ten Decades of Costume" each embroidered in an old-time oval framed picture design.

There are antique pieces, too, and these give meaning to the whole display. For what started the crafts of quilt and rug making but a hard pressed pioneer woman's determination to protect her family from the cold and to give her home such comfort as she could in a rough, new land?

Perhaps the first quilts in Canada were made without much thought for appearance. As in the year of "the great freeze" in Europe when people died from the cold as from a plague, our early settlers had a hard time to keep warm in their vulnerable log cabins. So the women took whatever heavy cloth they could find—pieces still intact in a man's worn overcoat, scraps of a worn-out blanket, joined these to make a bed-sized top and a lining and tacked the two together with yarn to make a "tied" quilt.

Even when these strictly utilitarian bed coverings gave way to quilts filled with batting or wool and topped with a patch-work of calico print, the patches were still scraps left over from the making of a woman's dress or a child's frock. It would have been considered rash extravagance to buy material to make a quilt. Perhaps there was thrift, too, in the way the early quilt patterns found a place for so many small pieces. A precious exhibit at the fair was a quilt-top pieced by a woman in the 1800's when she was over one hundred years old—a "Grandmother's Flower Bed" quilt made of the cotton print of the time, small patterned and mostly in such subdued colours as "cinnamon brown", buff and lilac—the last a staple colour for women's housedresses.

There was sentiment in the early craft of quilt making. A woman could tell where every patch came from—a family christening robe, someone's wedding dress. A girl pieced piles of quilts for her hope chest and sometimes her friends made her a special "bride's quilt." Women exchanged patterns and patches, especially pieces for the silk and velvet "throw" to drape over the back of a sofa—a "crazy-patched" creation elaborately decorated with embroidery stitching.

So quilts moved from humble, everyday necessities to things of style and elegance. Rugs had something of the same history. The first rug of the early settlers was a doormat for men to wipe the mud from their boots, but soon women found that homemade rugs could give their homes a touch of the colour and softness of carpets. They made their own designs—the overlapping half circles outlined from the heel of a man's shoe grew into the traditional and beautiful shell pattern. At the fair a very old mat of overlapping heel-shaped pieces of black and gray felt was only an aisle away from a hooked wall hanging, a picture so fine in line and colour blending that it might have been painted with a brush.

Artists at the fair talked a lot about colour, about harmony and warmth and "colours that leave you cold," as if colour was something that had been discovered yesterday, while right before us was a coverlet, woven over a hundred years ago, the yarn home-dyed in clear, strong red and blue and green and beige that came from weeds and bark and plants found in the locality. And these colours had not faded in well over a century.

So a quilt and rug fair must surely remind us that we are pensioners of the past. The women who worked so hard to create comfort and beauty and character in their homes, who took pride in the work of their hands, left a tradition which, happily, many women in these very different times seem to understand.

Cradle of Many Callings

The farm had been in the family for over a hundred years and the hard work and devotion of one generation after another had smoothed the fields and nourished the soil and planted trees to replace some of those uprooted in the first clearing. It was a place of lush meadows now, and good crops and fine buildings and people loyal to their calling—"a family of good farmers," the neighbours said. "It runs in the blood."

At a neighbourhood gathering to honour the century farm family, someone ventured to guess how many thousands of people had been fed from the farm over a hundred years, how much the family had given to the nation's economy. No one seemed to think of what the family had given the country, not only by way of good farming, but through its sons and daughters who had gone from the farm into other vocations.

When John Winter took the land from the Crown, it was an unbroken forest. He cut down trees, built a log cabin, brought his young wife from the Old Land and their children were born there. As his sons grew up they helped to clear the land and cultivate it, happy in pitting their strength against the forest and making a farm. Their mother taught them to read and write, for they had no school and few books; but John read to them from the Bible and young Andrew, by the time he was a man, knew half the Book by heart. He knew, too, that he was going to be a missionary. To send him to school was a hardship for all of them, but they were Scots and proud to have a minister in the family; and surely no student ever went through University with more frugality or dedication. Andrew gave his ministry to the lumber camps and mining towns of the West coast.

The farm expanded, the sons taking homesteads beside the original claim. A school was built and a sawmill. When there was an accident at the mill, a grandson of John Winter kept his head and took care of a gash in a man's leg so that the doctor who came the next day said he had saved an amputation and maybe a life. He looked at the boy's hands and told him what he wanted to hear—that he would make a surgeon. Again the family rose to the occasion and sent a son into Medicine.

A high school came to the county town, and while most of the Winter boys elected to stay on the land, a few of them and several girls who wanted to be teachers attended high school. After that the boys usually worked their way through university into law or engineering or, like their uncles, into medicine or the Church. As school teachers some of the girls were remembered years later for leading their pupils into ways they never could have found for themselves.

And while individuals of the clan distinguished themselves in other vocations, there were always brothers and sisters of the same mental calibre to stay with the farm. At one time they almost lost it, when the owner could see no need of giving his son a legal interest in it, and the boy left home and went West. There, with nothing to help him but the Winter determination and character and brains he "got ahead," made a place for himself in the new country and later represented his district in Parliament. It is said he was a good statesman.

As the father got older it seemed that the farm might have to be sold, but a daughter and her husband took it over and now their son carries on, saving the family tradition of good farming and adding some progressive measures of his own.

In the summing up, perhaps those who stayed on the home acres gave as much to the public good as those who went away; and perhaps the towns and cities could have supplied the men and women needed for work other than farming. But some of us who were country-bred had an idea that the Winters' country background was an asset wherever they were; that it gave them qualities needed in the city, too.

Today any Winter child can go to high school. Most of them find their vocations away from the farm since only a few are needed there. But whether they go or stay, country life has offered them special opportunities: to learn to work, to look in wonder at a starry sky or a rainbow, to search with compassion for a lost lamb or a new born calf, to run across the fields to see that the old neighbour living alone is all right, to stand up and be counted for their conviction if the need arises, to have an occasional quiet hour to think. It is our country's good fortune that farm life is the cradle for so many callings.

Overlooked

The social worker told a pathetic story of lost youth in the city; young people untrained to earn a living, taking whatever makeshift job they could find, never sure of steady employment; the lonely ones—some of them homeless, some in homes more lonely than the world outside; those who had drifted into bad company and a way of life they didn't like but felt unable to escape. There were the delinquents in trouble with the law; the unmarried girls in rescue homes waiting for their babies to be born; the emotionally disturbed, retreating into themselves or taking up with cults likely to leave them still more unbalanced; and the derelicts—girls walking the streets, youths sleeping in flop-houses among old men who had lost all hope of anything better.

It was a depressing picture and I hurried to explain how different things are in the country: boys and girls going through high school as a matter of course, children happily busy in 4H clubs, young people learning and growing and having a good time in church and young farmer groups. "Of course," I admitted, "this is life in the country. The young people a social worker sees have a city background." The social worker went back to her case histories. "Some of these came from the country," she said "—more of them than you might believe."

As I heard their stories I knew how easy it would be for the men and women, working with privileged farm children in their clubs and centres and churches, never to see the boy or girl on the fringe of these benefits or out of reach of them entirely. I began to see, too, that here and there, without any fuss about it, people are concerned about such children and are trying to help them.

In one of the best live stock areas of the country, everyone was proud of the boys' calf club—proud of the calves that took prizes at exhibitions but more proud of the boys themselves, eager, capable youngsters, growing in responsibility and so happy in their projects that second-rate interests weren't likely to attract them. No one seemed to think about the boy whose father either wasn't interested or couldn't afford to give him a calf to work with, or the boy at loose ends in the village, prospective recruit for a street gang because he had nothing better to do.

Then a new leader came along and started a club that any boy could join—a Conservation club. Boys from the village as well as the farms explored the woods, learned about wild life and soil and water, planted trees, lived in camps sometimes and discovered a new world, rugged and clean and as full of wonder as a piece of science fiction. Whatever the experience might mean to them later, there's no doubt it tided the "wild" ones over a time when they might snatch at any excitement; and that it gave a lift to those whose lives were dull and empty.

We are likely, too, to lose sight of our school drop-outs, boys and girls to be found later among the cities' unemployed. Betty Field was the oldest of a family of eight. They were poor and Betty decided to quit school and find a job in the city. With a few months' training in high school commerce and money to pay her first week's board at "the Y", she set out for a career in business.

Betty answered advertisements for a typist but her speed was not up to requirements. She tried for other office jobs but the employers wanted someone with experience. She went to an employment agency but with her lack of training they could offer nothing but a few days' work filling envelopes. At the agency she got into conversation with two girls a little older than herself, told them she didn't know how she was going to pay her next week's rent, and they invited her to move in with them.

This might have been a tragic experience. Fortunately Betty didn't like the way the girls lived or the friends who came to visit them. The next week she found another room, a room so cold and lonely that she could have wept for the little cubicle she had shared with her sisters at home. But she didn't think of going back—that would be letting the whole village know she had failed. Besides, she couldn't ask her mother to send the return fare and she hadn't an extra nickel of her own.

Back at home one of her teachers worried about Betty. She talked to her family, then wrote her and persisted until she made her see the stupidity of applying for work until she was trained for it. She persuaded her to come back to school. Then this teacher started a crusade to bring a commercial and trades school to the district to save rural youngsters, unequipped to take care of themselves, from going off to get lost in the city. A councillor argued that it was a waste of taxpayers' money to try to educate children who weren't steady enough to stay in school in the first place; but the teacher said, "These, too, are ours. We can't overlook them." (She might have added "And who knows how proud of them we may be some day?")

The Centennial Dress

The centennial dress brought it all back to me: the old house and the family and friends—not as they were quite a hundred years ago, but as far back as I could remember.

It was a beautiful dress with little red roses printed on a creamy calico, the sleeves long, the neckline high, the skirt full and the bodice fitting trimly. And the young woman who wore it stood very erect and stepped with dignity as girls were taught to do in the days when the dress was new. Wearing it, no girl would ever hook her knees over the arm of a chair or stand with one foot a yard from the other, like a runner ready to take off from first base. In a centennial dress a woman carried herself like a lady. Perhaps some day an inspired designer will find a way of working this grace into a chic new fashion.

The old house was a family house, large and rambling. And there were things about it that held the family together. In winter sometimes the kitchen was the only heated room so they all spent their leisure time there. On summer evenings they assembled on the front porch. All through the summer days the porch was a favourite spot with old people, and in its early years the house usually had grandparents on the premises —perhaps the older generation are in Rest Homes now. Anyway, the porch was taken away a few years ago when the picture windows were put in; at the same time the spare bedroom disappeared to give a larger living room. Evidently staying guests don't come any more.

Even without central heat or running water there was comfort in the old house. Bedrooms might be cold in winter but hot bricks and wool blankets made the beds warm. When a guest was expected the mattress was brought from the spare bed to "air" beside the parlour fire which, between company occasions, was always "laid" ready for lighting.

As I remember it, the parlour was not the much caricatured, gloomy show place, but a plush furnished, floral carpeted room with a piano, gilt-framed pictures and a centre table used mostly for a display of books—the Family Bible, the photograph album, a few school prizes, a profusely illustrated *Pilgrim's Progress*, and an anthology of *Well Loved Poems* bought from a travelling salesman. Perhaps the family did not often read these books but they stood for something they believed in, "gave a 'tone' to the place."

This "tone" was evident in other things about the house: in the handworked wall text, "God Bless Our Home," the starched pillow shams in the spare room, embroidered with "I Slept and Dreamed That Life Was Beauty," and "I Woke and Found That Life Was Duty"—amusing in these days, perhaps, but still saying something.

The gracious woman in the centennial dress revived memories of the hospitality in the home of her forebears—not the big family gatherings at Christmas and Thanksgiving, or the invitation dinners when the hostess brought out her best damask and silver and china and cooked the dishes for which she was famous. Without benefit of frozen artichokes or lettuce in mid-winter, these meals were feasts for the gods.

But the welcome seemed warmest for casual visitors. A neighbour passing on his way to the mill might drop his wife to spend the afternoon and call for her at supper time. Women took each other as they found them. "Now you won't go to any bother," the visitor begged and the hostess assured her that she wouldn't; but she usually added some festive item to the supper, such as a jar of her best preserves. A sort of ritual always went with the opening of the jar. Invariably the top was too tight for a woman to turn, so it was brought into the sitting room for the husband to open, which he did with apparently little effort and the dignity of a host in his own house. And how they talked! Is it true that we don't have much conversation any more because we would rather play bridge or watch television?

There was a snugness for both family and friends in the old house. (Fortunately they did not suffer the father domination too common a century ago.) And a home was a place for the family then—there was no radio or television constantly bringing the world into it. Of course we don't want to really escape from the world, nor have we any right to, but most of us need a little sanctuary somewhere. And as I looked at the young woman in the old-fashioned dress, it seemed that she might have the same capacity as her grandmothers for creating such a place. Perhaps she was already doing it in her own way.

The Clothesline

After forty years away from the place of her youth, Martha Newell crossed the continent to visit her old friend and neighbour, Mary Thorpe. As brides of the same year they had come to farms with only a road between. Now they found it good to relive the old days and to feel just as close in the new.

"You know what I'd like to do?" Martha said one day. "Do you remember, when we both had eggs to sell, we'd drive to town together and trade them in at the store? There were such nice farms and lovely homes all along the way—a drive I'll always remember. Could we take it again?"

Of course they could and they did. And if the farms had been thriving and the homes "lovely" forty years ago they might well be still more pleasing now, for the people loved their land; they had worked hard and intelligently; and the best new ways they could find had helped them.

"I miss something," Martha said as they drove along "—the clotheslines. You'll remember that for some reason the dealer wanted our eggs delivered on Monday mornings. This is Monday too, but you'd never know it. There isn't a washing in sight. When we drove past these places forty years ago it was like watching a movie. The clothes on a line practically told you who lived there. Out West a woman who had almost lost her mind from loneliness, on a homestead, told me that on one of her rare trips to town, past the usual bachelors' shacks, she suddenly cried out as if she had seen a vision. On a line from a shack to the stable a row of little white squares flapped in the wind. There was another woman in the district, and a baby!

They remembered the tremendous washings young mothers had to do when little girls and women too, wore starched dresses and pettitcoats and pinafores. They spoke of the winter washdays in the years when everyone wore long woollen underthings that froze stiff and jigged in the wind like puppets on a string. "I used to heat the clothespins in the oven so my fingers wouldn't freeze before I got everything on the line," Martha recalled. "And sometimes," Mary added "you'd have half a dozen sheets still stiff as boards when you went to bring them in at night. Once one got away from me in a high wind and went skittering across the yard over the fence and into a snow drift across the road."

"Still," Martha persisted, "even in winter there was something about a clothesline. It told you that life went on in the house, a woman was caring for her family. It was part of country living. Don't the women around here do such work at home any more?"

"Sure they do," Mary said, "but most of them have dryers—clothes dryers, you know; they save carrying baskets of wet clothes as well as going out in all weathers."

"I've used one for years," Martha said, "but I wouldn't have expected to find them on farms."

Then, up the road they actually saw a washing on a line—a half dozen blankets, blue and pink and mauve and yellow. "Lovely!" Martha exclaimed. "A study in pastels! At our art exhibit there was a picture of a white house with hollyhocks and a lineful of clothes repeating the colours in the flowers—a delightful subject. I wonder more painters haven't thought of it. Why, that must be Nellie's place! Trust her. I'll bet as long as she lives she'll have a clothesline."

"I shouldn't wonder," Mary agreed, "even if she only uses it to fluff out her blankets in the spring."

"That's just it," Martha said. "Who wouldn't want to dry clothes out doors in air as clean as this?"

"But," Mary went on, "when her son's baby was born last winter, Nellie saw to it there was a dryer in the house when her daughter-in-law came home from the hospital."

"I suppose she was right," Martha admitted. "Just the same, I miss the clotheslines. So much that made the country the place I like to remember seems to be disappearing."

"I know what you mean," Mary said. "Last summer an artist came through here looking for a field of stooked wheat. He couldn't find one anywhere. The combine had taken all that beauty away. I was sorry about the picture; but I'm not sorry that men now don't have to trudge across a field carrying sheaves of wheat all day, or smother in the dust of a barn threshing.

"A couple down the road from us like to sing," Mary continued, "but for years their chores have kept them working so late they couldn't even get to choir practice. Now with some new machinery to ease their work they've joined a choral club. But passersby won't see a lighted barn at nine o'clock, sign that a farmer in the good old tradition is getting his cattle settled for the night, the last thing before he goes to bed himself.

"I suppose the country is losing a sort of colour," Mary considered; "but perhaps we're going to have more time and more spirit for other kinds of colour—such as a choral club."

In Spring We Remember

From her window the woman looked over the fields to the woods at the back of the farm. "Already you can see spring coming," she said, "—days lengthening, the sun stronger, a yellow fuzz on the willows even with snow still in the hollows. So much that some of us loved about the country is disappearing; but every year brings seedtime and harvest, and each new season—perhaps especially spring—stirs such nostalgia for the old ways that we never let them die out completely.

"Spring begins for me when I find the seed catalogues in the mailbox," the woman went on. "Even if the cold is below zero, here is something to warm the day—a splash of summer flowers across the cover and growing things on every page inside. I think of the garden I will make. I see the tangle of colour, hear the bees humming, feel the wonder of going out in the morning to see what flowers have come in the night. Just so my pioneer grandmother must have felt when she trained morning-glories up the walls of her log cabin, planted hollyhocks to screen the wood-pile, and bleeding hearts and bachelor's buttons in the front yard. As long as a country woman can have her flowers, the country is still the country.

The woman told about the big kitchen garden that had once given the family something of a gourmand's table. Now the men said it cost less to buy vegetables than to grow them. But the woman felt this wasn't the same at all; so she has a little plot that she cultivates herself, "just enough for a meal or two of everything when it's new." She said: "Remember the spring evenings when we used to take the lantern out to the garden and pull a few green onions for a bedtime snack? We still do that—with a flashlight."

The hunger for something green in spring she thought might be a hangover from the days when, at the end of a hard winter, an old woman would say to her doctor, "I'll be all right as soon as I can get out and pick me a mess of greens." She herself doesn't gather "greens," but she said, "I do get watercress from our creek every spring and I make quite a ceremony of the first rhubarb pie. Though we don't make maple syrup any more, this is the time of year when we have maple syrup and johnny cake—just old farm customs."

There were other things that hadn't changed with the changing ways of farming. The woman said: "Fortunately the clatter of tractors and the poison sprays on the crops haven't driven the birds away. Year after year they come back. When the orchard had to go—another concession to specialized farming —many nesting sites went with the old trees. That was when we started setting up bird houses. So long as the birds come back in spring we know we're still in the country.

"And just as dependable as the spring freshets in the creeks and the dandelions on the lawn, out come little girls' skipping ropes and little boys' marbles. This happens in town, too; but there are other children's games that seem to belong to the country. A few years ago when we drove past our one-room school at recess, we saw the children playing 'Duck on the Rock' and 'Run Sheep Run' and 'Prisoner's Base'. Do they play these timeless old games at the township schools now, or just organized sports? I don't know," the woman said. "But when my grandchildren and their friends come here to play, it may be that I drop a word about an old game that gets them started, but anyway they never seem to tire of them. I hear the old calls and chants and it might be my own children playing out there or even myself and my friends in a time still farther away."

The little country church had closed years ago, the woman told me, but it still stood in the graveyard that served the community even yet, and every spring they had a memorial service there. Families nearby came on Saturday night to cut the grass and trim the shrubs and on Sunday they brought baskets of flowers; and there were always enough for the graves of those whose families were far away now. In the evening the one service of the year was held in the old church. Visitors came from far and near; they loitered beside family plots, exchanged memories and inquired for old friends. And when the old bell rang, the pews were filled again as they had been fifty years ago. For one short hour country ways had not changed. Sunset colours played on the walls, the choir loft bloomed with syringa and lilacs, the tinkle of a sheep bell or the bleat of a lamb might come in at the open windows; and— surest of all signs of spring and renewal—

> Over heads devoutly bowed
> Young lovers' eyes were shouting.

The woman said, "There's so much in spring to make us remember."